His Initials Were F.D.N.

On his tour of the Near East, F. D. N. is seen here climbing the Tomb
of Cyrus, near Persepolis, Persia (Iran).

His Initials Were
F. D. N.

A Life Story of Elder F. D. Nichol,
for twenty-one years
editor of the Review and Herald

By
Miriam and Kenneth Wood

Published and Copyrighted © 1967 by the
Review and Herald Publishing Association

Library of Congress Catalog Card No. 67-21872

OFFSET IN U.S.A.

Dedication

To Seventh-day Adventists all over the world who felt the influence of F. D. N.'s pen, but did not have the opportunity to know him personally, as we did, this book is dedicated.

—The Authors

THE NICHOL FAMILY

At the right is Elder F. D. Nichol with his father, mother, and two sisters, Mary Jane and Dorothy. Mary Jane (left) is the only survivor.

Contents

Acknowledgments

In writing this book we have been indebted to a large number of people. First and foremost to Mrs. F. D. Nichol, whose ability to put aside her grief and open the door to all the past years was truly remarkable. The Nichols' only child, Virginia Saxon, "shared" her father with us generously; as did Mary Jane Nichol, Elder Nichol's sister. Dr. Alonzo L. Baker wrote such a sparkling record of the *Signs of the Times* years that we were tempted to publish it exactly as he had written it! Arthur L. White, Don Neufeld, Raymond Cottrell, T. K. Martin, Carolyn Eells Keeler, Jewell Peeke, John Loor, William Loveless, Julia Neuffer, Frederick Lee, Zetta Brown, Thelma Wellman, Edna Edeburn, Mrs. Nellie S. Rockwell, and many others contributed incidents and insights.

Promise Joy Sherman and Janet Faye Minesinger typed the manuscript.

Our heartfelt thanks to all these wonderful people.

THE AUTHORS

"I will drink
Life to the lees. . . .
How dull it is to pause, to make an end,
To rust unburnish'd, not to shine in use! . . .
Life piled on life
Were all too little."

—ALFRED, LORD TENNYSON
"Ulysses"

Francis David Nichol in 1955.

Foreword

Throughout the Adventist world, wherever the *Review and Herald* goes, the initials of the *Review* editors become familiar to readers—almost as familiar as the initials of their own families. Many Adventists play a kind of game—trying to guess the author of an editorial before looking for the initials. So intimately connected have initials been with the weekly habit of reading the *Review*, that once, in 1955, when the editors decided to use no initials with their editorials, readers protested mightily. Some threatened to cancel their subscriptions. Not surprisingly, in less than five months the editors capitulated and restored the initials.

For the twenty-one years that Francis David Nichol was editor in chief, and for the preceding seventeen that he was an associate editor, the initials F. D. N. appeared at the end of *Review* editorials. A whole generation of readers grew up reading the incisive writing of this great and good man. The initials F. D. N. were a kind of hallmark on an editorial or article, assuring the reader of high quality in content and style.

Thus when Francis David Nichol died suddenly on June 3, 1966, Adventists all over the world felt personally bereaved. During the succeeding months the absence of Elder Nichol's editorials in the *Review* accompanied by the familiar initials F. D. N. heightened the sense of personal loss.

We hope that this book will to some extent fill the void left by the missing initials. Throughout the book, except where we are writing about his early years, we refer to Elder Nichol as F. D. N. In the same way we use the initials R. F. C. and K. H. W. to refer to Raymond F. Cottrell and Kenneth H.

9

Wood, Elder Nichol's associate editors in recent years. To make the book easier to read and follow, we have used the personal pronoun "I" to refer to K. H. W., even though the writing has been a joint project.

As we gathered material for this book we were inspired anew by the many-faceted life of F. D. N. Every new probe deepened our conviction that here indeed was a brilliant, unique, and dedicated man, a man whose life story would inspire young and old alike.

We have not attempted to write a definitive biography, only a human-interest story. Nor have we endeavored to be entirely objective. Quite frankly, we admired and loved F. D. N., and this bias is apparent—we hope. We believe, however, that we have pictured him as he really was—a colorful man of great talents, whom God used mightily to advance the Advent Movement.

Miriam G. Wood
Kenneth H. Wood

10

CHAPTER 1

Prologue

FOR ME, the story of Francis David Nichol began in his *Review* office on a raw, windy day early in November, 1955. Elder Nichol had invited me to come for an interview, and to bring my wife with me. Now we were sitting there listening to this man, whom we had always held somewhat in awe, asking me to join the staff of the *Review and Herald*.

I can still see the office as it was that day, as doubtless it had been for many years. It contained two desks, one of which faced the east wall, on which hung nearly a score of enlarged snapshots of archeological ruins. F. D. N. had visited these places in the Bible lands on one of his world tours. As proof, one needed only to note various poses of him in front of crumbling pillars, ruined amphitheaters, and weather-beaten sculptures.

My inspection of the office came to an abrupt halt as F. D. N., in what I came to know as his let's-get-on-with-the-job-and-have-no-nonsense approach, launched into his description of what the job of a *Review* editor involved.

"I want you to know, young man"—and this was the first time I was addressed in this way, but only the first time, since F. D. N. considered all his younger associates as mere callow youths—"I want you to know that there's nothing glamorous about this job. Some people have the mistaken idea that editorial work is easy—even fun. Nothing could be farther from the truth. It's work, work, work, and grind, grind, grind."

When he paused for a moment I found my eyes riveted on the wall opposite his second desk (he sat in a high-backed swivel chair between the two desks, so that he could work at

11

PAINTING BY HARRY ANDERSON

"ASCENSION" BY HARRY ANDERSON

The original of this picture hung in the editorial office of Elder Nichol.
It still hangs there in the office of his successor.

either one), where hung a weird devil mask, which I later learned he had brought from New Guinea. On the near wall was a boomerang from Australia, and from the Philippines a black, wooden shield covered with little silver swords.

During moments of high drama in life most of us, I suppose, remember small details with almost blinding clarity; I felt a positive intimacy with the mask, the boomerang, and the shield on this, my first sight of them!

"Yes, indeed," F. D. N. continued, "up here on the third floor we have a superabundance of dull routine. You can't publish a paper any other way."

He wanted to make certain that I would take up my new responsibility with absolutely no illusions as to what the job involved, and what my probable sufferings would be. He painted an alarming picture of what predicaments I might face, particularly as regards editorial writing.

"There'll be times," he said, "when you'll have to write an editorial—you'll absolutely *have* to write one—and there you'll sit, staring at the four walls, with not even the glimmer of an idea in your head. Worse than that, you'll feel that the possibility of *ever* having another idea is extremely remote!"

He spoke with such deep feeling that it was obvious he had had the experience himself, although I had never imagined him as anything but completely fluent, full of ideas just flowing off the end of his pen, typewriter, or dictating machine. I glanced at my wife, to see if she had grasped this surprising revelation, but her eyes were riveted on Harry Anderson's painting, *The Ascension,* on the far wall. I knew she was doing some pretty serious thinking herself, but she was doing it silently, being somewhat awestruck.

Having ascertained that I was unintimidated by the job he was offering me, F. D. N. asked what my reaction had been when he telephoned me the preceding day in Cleveland, Ohio,

THREE WELL-KNOWN *REVIEW AND HERALD* EDITORS—
W. A. Spicer, F. D. Nichol, F. M. Wilcox. Taken at the General Conference, 1946, in Takoma Park, Maryland.

PROLOGUE

where I was attending a Dorcas Federation meeting as a departmental secretary in the Columbia Union. "Tell me, Brother-r-r Wood," he began slowly, extending the ending consonants, as if he were rather pleased with the Scotch-Irish sound of it all, "how you felt when I talked to you yesterday." He leaned his head back in a typical pose, against the back of the extremely high-backed swivel chair that was one of his trademarks. This chair, "inherited" from his predecessor, Elder F. M. Wilcox, was one of Elder Nichol's most highly prized possessions.

I assured him that I was thrilled, excited, entirely certain that this was an assignment I had always hoped for—that words were inadequate to describe my sensations. He seemed pleased. I explained that although I had worked nearly eighteen years as an evangelist, pastor, and departmental secretary, my first love was the publishing business; that as a young man in academy and college I had learned the printing trade, and had edited the college paper and annual.

F. D. N. smiled. Well he knew that all of this was a far cry from being an editor of the *Review*.

During a momentary pause in the conversation my gaze riveted on the two walls full of books—theology, sociology, history, literature—anything and everything was there. I longed to get my hands on them.

And next to F. D. N. was another trademark, a cube-shaped swivel bookcase on wheels, containing his most-used reference books.

I then looked back at F. D. N.'s piercing blue eyes behind his shiny rimless glasses (never was I able, in the following ten years, to persuade him to wear horn rims).

"We've been fortunate in the *Review*," he said, as he put his finger tips together, leaned back, and closed his eyes; "we've never had an editor involved in a moral lapse or heresy—even though not all have agreed on all points of doctrine." Fasten-

15

ing my eyes on the large plants and ferns in front of the window, I examined my conscience. Finding it clear on both counts, I prepared to listen further.

"Our people depend on the *Review*. They have faith in it. They feel that it is solid, that they can trust it. I wouldn't want that ever to change, or anyone to be associated with the paper who would want to change that," he went on, firmly.

Lost in thought, he paused for a moment. There was only the clank of a radiator and the distant sound of an elevator to break the stillness. Then, with an abrupt change of mood so characteristic of him, F. D. N. asked, "Well, when can you start?"

I gained the distinct impression that I should have started yesterday, but I suggested that perhaps I could start in about three weeks. I pointed out that the Columbia Union would need to find a new departmental secretary.

"That'll be fine!" he exclaimed. He was deeply immersed in the massive project of producing *The SDA Bible Commentary*, working literally night and day. D. A. Delafield, one of his associates on the *Review*, had just accepted an invitation to join the White Publications office, and F. D. N. needed another editor to assist Elder Frederick Lee, his long-time associate.

On December 1, 1955, I reported to the *Review* office. The work was all that F. D. N. had said it would be—routine, exacting, and unglamorous. And there *were* days when I thought I had run out of ideas worth putting on paper. But the job offered something that compensated for it all—the friendship of F. D. N., a friendship that has left a lasting influence on my life. And I found work that to me was the most satisfying I had ever done.

It began, then, on a November day in 1955. That beginning and that friendship set in motion the chain of events that eventually produced this book.

CHAPTER 2

F.D.N., Editor of the Review

FOR THE last twenty-one years of his life, F. D. N. was editor of the *Review and Herald,* the official church paper of the Seventh-day Adventists. He loved the *Review* and all that it represented. So satisfying to him was his post as editor that he was tempted to pity people who had to be content with other jobs. The danger and power resident in the printed word fascinated him, and the potential for helping others inspired him.

Tilting back in his distinctive chair, he endeavored on various occasions to impart his enthusiasm to his associates. "The *Review and Herald,*" he would intone impressively, "has but one purpose—to build up the saints in the most holy faith."

Incidentally, F. D. N. wasn't the least bit squeamish about using the word "saint." Feeling that those who are committed to Christ and Present Truth have a right to the title, he termed his flock "saints"—even those with flagrant faults.

The solemn responsibility of editing the *Review* weighed heavily on him at all times, but his sense of humor reveled in the everyday happenings and predicaments on the purely human level of frailty.

In dealing with his associates, for example, he operated a kind of mythical point system of the "heads I win, tails you lose" variety. He deducted points from anyone who made a mistake, however trifling. A small mistake could cost five points. A big mistake could run as high as fifty points, and a

2

REVIEW AND HERALD BUILDING

The flag flies at half-mast in respectful tribute to the memory of Elder F. D. Nichol, editor of the *Review and Herald* for 21 years.

really first-class, king-sized "blooper" might go into multiples of fifty. Failure to spot a typographical error on a page proof would elicit a crisp, "That'll cost you five points, young man!" A theological error would produce a sober head-wagging announcement of doom: "You've just lost fifty points!"

The odd thing about F. D. N.'s point system was that five points was usually the maximum awarded for superior performance, while fifty points was the common deduction for a slip-up. For example, once I caught a grammatical error in F. D. N.'s editorial, and was greeted with, "Well, I'll give you five points for that. You'll be needing them." How right he

18

was! Later, when I let a misspelled word get through, I lost fifty points.

His associates didn't take the point system too seriously, yet there was an element of challenge in it! Never will I forget that I lost a multiple of fifty points at one blow several years ago for some carelessly worded statements in an editorial on women's dress. As the irate letters began to pour in, F. D. N. used to come into my office and chortle, "Well, that'll teach you, young man!"

R. F. C.* suffered a similar fate because of an editorial that some readers felt was an endorsement of a certain political candidate. Again the fifty-point deduction.

F. D. N. was quite likely gleefully to point out to his crestfallen younger associates that "the pen is mightier than the sword and a lot easier to become impaled upon"—which didn't help alleviate their sufferings.

Another of F. D. N.'s cardinal editorial rules was his "check and double check" requirement. The idea of leaving anything to chance was so repugnant to him that it better never be suggested in his presence. Dates? Check twice, three times, four times, with the proper people. Initials? Check with every available source. Strolling into the paste-up room, where the dummy was being put together, he'd often glance down a column, then inquire, "Did you call the General Conference secretarial department on those dates?"

"Yes indeed; just as you've taught us," would be the reply.

Then he'd wander out, shaking his head and murmuring just loudly enough to be heard, "Well, I certainly hope the dates are right. We can't afford a mistake like that——" and so on until he was out of earshot.

With this stringent attention to accuracy, there was little margin for error. But, alas, the publishing business is a perilous pursuit. Upon one occasion F. D. N. had written an edito-

---

* For explanation of initials, see Foreword, page 9.

rial that contained near the end the Scripture quotation, "They loved not their lives unto the death." It went through the copyroom, the proofroom, the typeroom—*all* the rooms—correctly; but an alert pressman, idly reading a spoiled sheet, suddenly noticed that the line read, "They loved not their *wives* unto the death"!

Immediately the press was stopped and the error corrected. Someone, in correcting another error in the line, had inadvertently misspelled "lives" as "wives." (It is better that the perpetrator's name remain in the halls of anonymity; far better.) F. D. N. writhed in humiliation over this "blooper."

Another day that will live in infamy is the day that an entire issue of the *Review* was published with an article that had no beginning. In those days the *Review* was run one-half at a time, in two forms. The first form went to press several days before the second form which included the cover and the back page, as well as half the "inside." Articles were not run from one form to another, so that late news could be inserted at the last minute in the second form without affecting the first form.

Occasionally F. D. N. would come striding purposefully down the hall to either R. F. C.'s or my office, waving a story that he thought was important enough to warrant remaking several pages of the second form.

On the aforementioned infamous day, at the last moment it was decided that an entire story should be lifted out and another substituted. Possible? With a quick glance at the forms, one of the associates gave an affirmative answer. The story was lifted out—so R. F. C. and I thought! We continued in our dream world until Mrs. Nichol, a most avid and interested reader of the *Review,* was going through her copy on Friday night.

"What in the world is this?" she inquired of her trying-to-relax husband, pointing to several columns of type that were no part of either the article that preceded or the one that followed.

With his heart in his mouth (an occupational disease that often afflicts editors) F. D. N. took the paper from her hands and inspected it carefully—not once, but repeatedly.

Could it be? It could. It was. In lifting out the story, only the first two pages had been removed. Its ending, on the third page, had simply been overlooked. There it sat, a monument to a moment of carelessness.

Heads didn't exactly roll, but points surely did! Multiples of fifty were deducted from everybody even remotely connected with the boner. Grimly, F. D. N. asked that the story be run again, this time undecapitated. A few weeks later this was done. Interestingly, not a single letter was received regarding this dreadful blunder. There was much conjecture on the part of the three editors as to the reason for this. "We were lucky," the editor declared solemnly. He also assured his younger associates that people are quick to forget. "Even when a reader does spot a mistake, he doesn't remember it long." He was right, of course.

Related to F. D. N.'s editorial principles was his firm conviction that election to office, political, religious, or whatever, does not make a man great. In his opinion, a man must be great apart from election. "Winston Churchill," he was fond of saying, "would be a great man whether in or out of office; he proved it."

It followed, then, that he felt obligated to help his associates realize their full potential—to realize *more* than their potential, as a matter of fact. Rather typical was his habit of coming into R. F. C.'s office or mine waving a letter from a subscriber, the letter containing justifiable criticism.

"Do you have a minute?" was his invariable opening question. Upon being assured that the minute was available (naturally), he often began like this:

F. D. N. standing at his office desk, 1949, at the time he was writing the book *Ellen G. White and Her Critics*.

F. D. N., EDITOR OF THE *REVIEW*

"I want to use this letter as a text to make a point. I don't know of any other way to bring this to your attention. . . ."

Then he would go on to show how the particular incident could have been handled differently, or how the mistake could have been avoided.

"You see," he'd conclude, "I won't be here forever, and I want to make you men the very best editors that I can."

One editorial procedure at which he excelled was the task of revising a paragraph after the copy was already in type. Putting his enormous verbal skills to work, he was able to change a word here or a phrase there so that only one or two lines at best would have to be reset.

"This kind of thing saves the house money," was his explanation for the extra mental effort involved. ("The house," of course, was the Review and Herald Publishing Association.)

A similar evidence of thrift was revealed in his relation with the copyroom. Since all factual material must be verified by the copy editors, he'd often write the words "For copy editors only" in the margin of his editorials, then he'd give the sources of statistics or quotations. This saved valuable time for the copy editors—and money for the house.

The extreme care with which F. D. N. worked was evidenced even in his handwriting. When I first joined the staff, and began to edit manuscripts, I noted the beautifully written editorial changes here and there in the articles. I had learned to recognize the handwriting of Elder Frederick Lee, F. D. N.'s long-time associate editor, and knew that he had not made the changes. It was some time before I discovered that the clear, legible changes were the work of F. D. N. himself. Feeling that my own handwriting suffered distinctly by comparison, I derived a small crumb of comfort from the fact that F. D. N. never got around to dotting his "i's"!

According to his own admission, F. D. N. acquired from Elder Wilcox a strong aversion to procrastination. One result was that he always wrote his editorials far ahead of deadlines. He'd shut himself in his office on Friday afternoons and Sundays, writing, writing, writing, to build up a good reserve. Then at the opportune moment he'd present a dozen or so to his associates, with the justifiably self-righteous comment, "Here are my editorials for the next three months." With a twinkle in his eyes, he'd clear his throat, and add, "I just thought this might keep you on your toes."

He was not at all averse to enjoying hugely the figurative gnashing of teeth that this remark engendered in the souls of associates who were editorial-less just a few hours ahead of the deadline.

F. D. N. was greatly in demand as a speaker, particularly for formal occasions such as commencement exercises, anniversary celebrations, and departmental advisory councils. Some speakers might wait until the last minute to prepare. Not F. D. N. He set himself a firm deadline to have his message fully prepared and mastered at least one month ahead of the appointment.

And he labored over these addresses with tireless patience, polishing them to high luster. His first draft would usually go to his associates and others whose counsel he valued. Sometimes the response was merciless, but if the criticisms seemed valid, he immediately set about to make the necessary revisions. If he decided the criticisms were not valid, he defended his position stoutly.

Sometimes, in the last years, he would read aloud portions of an address he was working on, inviting his associates to suggest more effective ways of presentation. Often he warmed to his subject as he read, gesticulating with his arms (at least the one that wasn't holding the manuscript!), his voice becoming louder and louder. His associates enjoyed it; so did he.

The steady stream of visitors to his office he regarded with mixed emotions. His work, both assigned and self-imposed, was tailored to perhaps a thirty-six-hour day. Yet, if possible, he put aside pressing tasks for a rewarding chat. Occasionally, when committee meetings or other time-consuming activities put him under unusual pressure, he'd close his office door—firmly and with finality. Several times I arrived just after he'd barricaded himself in this way.

"I just must ask him something," I'd explain to Promise Sherman, his secretary.

Mrs. Sherman, the soul of tact and kindness, would hesitate, torn between her instructions and her inclinations.

"Is it extremely important?" she'd ask. "You see, he told me to hang out the 'leprosy' sign." He'd keep the figurative "leprosy" sign up until he accomplished enough work to feel less tense, then he'd once more become available to visitors.

Visitors, incidentally, reached the editor not only in person but by mail—through a never-ending stream of letters, approving, criticizing, suggesting, despairing, flattering, commenting, pleading. If every writer who had dashed his missive off in all its ungrammatical muddiness and illegible handwriting could have seen the care with which F. D. N. read it, he might have felt a few twinges of conscience about putting an added strain on so busy a man.

Each signed letter received courteous attention, and a careful reply. If the letter expressed criticism, and F. D. N. decided that the criticism was justified, he thanked the correspondent for his interest. If the criticism could have been avoided by greater care on the part of his editorial associates, he'd call the matter to their attention. "How in the world did this get by?" he'd exclaim, then offer a sermonet on how to do better in the future.

Correspondents who contended with him over a long period of time discovered that he was a formidable defender of his position—and an untiring one. Carefully he'd analyze their doctrinal mistakes, their warped interpretations, their misinformation, sometimes for three and four single-spaced typewritten pages. Pastoral work this certainly was, above and beyond the call of duty. I used to ask him why he didn't just ignore some of the more obviously contentious letters.

"Some of these people may have no one else to talk to; and they have souls to save," he'd reply firmly.

If correspondents were glaringly in error, he took a modicum of Christian joy in putting them to rout, his logic and rhetoric overwhelming them to the extent that these unfortunates seldom cared to prolong the contest.

As for anonymous letters, he gave them the standard editorial treatment, promptly and decisively. They were put into the "circular file"—the wastebasket, that is.

Among the honors that came to F. D. N. while he was the *Review* editor was a D.D. degree from Andrews University in 1958.* He was the first man to receive this degree from that institution (while it was still Potomac University). His associates on third floor decided that this was a fine opportunity

---

* See Appendix D for citation read by C. E. Weniger.

F. D. N. receiving his D.D. degree from E. D. Dick, president of the SDA Theological Seminary, during graduating exercises held in the Takoma Park church.

for a practical joke. Enlisting the aid of art department personnel, they had a new sign prepared for F. D. N.'s office door. Before he arrived the next morning the sign was properly installed—"F. D. Nichol, D.D., Editor."

When F. D. N. appeared on the scene, the practical jokers were standing around to observe his reaction. Someone called his attention to the "D.D." and chided him on becoming "puffed up" over the new honor he had received. Looking at the sign, he good-naturedly exclaimed, "Who in the world did that? Take it out and don't let me ever catch sight of it again!" The somewhat chastened practical jokers removed the sign promptly and restored the old one that said, simply, "F. D. Nichol, Editor."

With a modesty that some people never suspected, F. D. N. consistently discouraged people from calling him "Doctor," though he had every right to the title. He seemed ill at ease when someone, perhaps in making an introduction, used the term.

He also seemed ill at ease whenever he was the center of a social event—for example, when his birthday was being celebrated—but he enjoyed hugely the celebrations for others. Occasionally just before noon, or a few minutes before quitting time in the evening, the personnel on third floor would have ice cream and cake to celebrate a birthday. F. D. N. almost always was present. He never ate much—he was spartan with himself in these situations—but he enjoyed himself enormously, telling appropriate stories and teasing the birthday person unmercifully. "The life of the party" was F. D. N.

Those who knew him intimately always thought that F. D. N. would have reveled in the editorship of a large metropolitan daily newspaper, had his energies not been dedicated to the spreading of the gospel. He could hardly wait for each General Conference session, when the daily Bulletins were issued. He loved to have the plant running on a twenty-four-hour-a-day basis, with all the accompanying excitement and tension.

His first experience with the Bulletins came at the editorially tender age of twenty-five, in 1922, when a combination of emergency circumstances caused him to be asked to report the conference. At that time he was one of the editors of the *Signs of the Times* in Mountain View, California. General Conference was being held in San Francisco, some thirty-eight miles away. Little did he suspect that he would be intimately connected with the Bulletins for every session during the next forty-four years!

Preplanning—that was the secret of making the Bulletin program work smoothly. Schedules. Who would work at the plant as secretaries? Who would go to General Conference to work? Who would keep the daily log of each event at the conference? Who would write the daily story? What time would copy be sent to Washington—by air mail and telephone?

Except for the 1936 session, when some material was sent by teletype, the telephone was the chief medium of news transmission. A special telephone, hooked up to the recording machine in Washington, was installed.

I used to enjoy watching and listening to F. D. N. as he did his telephone dictation each evening about six o'clock. There he'd sit, in our temporary office a few steps from the arena where the General Conference was in session, the telephone receiver to his ear, repeating with exaggerated distinctness, " 'A' as in Adam, 'D' as in David—did you get that? . . ." and so on and on, speaking with theatrical slowness. He was not above a bit of showmanship every now and then!

With unconcealed anticipation he was looking forward to the use of the TWX machines that, in 1966, transmitted all Bulletin material on tapes at one hundred words per minute, typing the copy simultaneously in Detroit and in Takoma Park, thus making obsolete the former telephone system. But he

F. D. N. sending copy for the General Conference Bulletin by long-distance telephone from San Francisco to Washington, 1941. Ruth Conard and Dr. Charles E. Weniger were assisting.

Editorial group at 1941 General Conference examining first issue of the GC Bulletin from the Review and Herald office. C. E. Palmer, F. D. Nichol, F. M. Wilcox, Frederick Lee, and Charles E. Weniger.

never saw it in operation. It was with tight throats and suspiciously moist eyes that the crew transmitted the first messages of the session. "How he'd have loved to see those tapes running through like lightning!" one person after another remarked, over and over.

Months before each General Conference session, F. D. N. wrote to all who would be giving reports—heads of divisions, departments, institutions, et cetera. In 1966 he sent the following letter to all concerned:

"January 13, 1966

"Dear Brother _____:

"This is to request that you provide me not later than April 1 with a report for the General Conference Bulletin on the work of your department. This report should be not more than three typewritten pages, double spaced, in harmony with the decision on space limits that was set up by a special committee. Please note carefully the time this manuscript is due. We must adhere rigidly to this schedule. Kindly send to Elder W. R. Beach a copy of the report you prepare for me.

"Sincerely,

"F. D. Nichol

"P.S. Please be sure to sign and return the enclosed post card. I want to be doubly sure that each of you has received my letter informing you of your writing assignment for the Bulletin."

And the enclosed card, no nonsense about it, read as follows:

"Dear Brother Nichol:

"I will plan to have my report in your hands by April 1, and will send a carbon copy to W. R. Beach.

"Signed _____"

The method worked perfectly. All the reports were in hand in plenty of time to be set before the session began.

F. D. N. holding up edition of Bulletin announcing the election of W. H. Branson to the General Conference presidency.

Part of the Review and Herald Bulletin staff at the 1962 General Conference at San Francisco. Standing back of Elder Nichol (seated) are T. K. Martin, Lawrence Maxwell, H. M. Tippett, Promise Sherman, R. F. Cottrell, M. R. Thurber, Vada Gentry, Areta Perkins, Byron Logan, Ray Hanna.

In spite of the fact that the reports were standing, ready to appear in the Bulletin, the associate editor at the plant was kept in a state of constant terror lest a slip-up occur. F. D. N. never let him forget that if anything went wrong, "the brethren will fire me because they won't know who did it, but I'll fire you because I'll know who did."

When the first Bulletin arrived at each General Conference session, F. D. N. with considerable flourish, took pardonable pride in presenting it to the General Conference president. He liked to remind the delegates that if they *really* wanted to know what was going on, they'd better read the daily *Review* Bulletins!

F. D. N. had almost a reverence for the publishing work. The printed page, to him so permanent and far reaching, was an object to be approached with great care. This may have been the result of his parents' spectacular conversion (which we shall recount in chapter 13). Or it may have been his natural love of the intellectual stimulation that books and magazines offer. Whatever the reason, many times during the daily eight o'clock worship on third floor he prayed for a blessing "on this house and its products."

The very peril of the publishing business made it doubly exhilarating to F. D. N. Since the occasional errors that crept in, regardless of the check-and-double-check system, gave his brethren "across the way" (in the General Conference building) an opportunity to tease him good-naturedly, one would have thought that perhaps he would have preferred a safer kind of job.

Not F. D. N.! One day on the sidewalk, a General Conference fellow worker asked with gentle banter, "Are you still living dangerously there at the Review?"

"Yes," F. D. N. flashed back, "and by God's grace we shall continue to do so!"

Correlated with his strong feeling about publishing was

his firm belief in literature evangelism. In morning worships his prayers nearly always contained a reference to the literature evangelists and their important work. "O God, give them the strength and courage to meet the public successfully today." If all the literature evangelists, in small towns and big cities, in the country and metropolitan areas, could have visualized him there, his head bowed reverently, praying for them, I think they would have made their house-to-house visits with new courage.

Elder F. M. Wilcox, who'd been F. D. N.'s "chief" from 1928 to 1944, was to the latter an ideal to be emulated, to be quoted, to be loved.* He often claimed that "all I know about editorial work I learned from Elder Wilcox."

One rule that F. D. N. adopted from Elder Wilcox and passed along to us was, "When in doubt about publishing something—*don't!*" Many times during my ten years with F. D. N. the chief made this comment. Then shaking his head for emphasis, he would usually add—"Don't forget, young man; they can't shoot you for what you don't publish." A mental picture of the editorial firing squad in action was usually enough to subdue even the most headstrong younger associates.

Occasionally, when either R. F. C. or I pressed a suggestion that we considered particularly good, and F. D. N. was dubious about its merit but hesitant to give a negative response, he'd lean back in his chair, fold his hands across his chest, and look meditatively toward the ceiling. "This is a judgment on me," he'd murmur, with pseudo-meekness. "I realize now what a terrible torment I must have been to Elder Wilcox. I'm being punished by having two young associates with 'bright' ideas," and he'd glance mischievously about him to see whether his words were having the proper effect.

Whatever he may have said in private by way of rebuke

---

* See Appendix B for F. D. N.'s tribute to Elder Wilcox, read at his funeral and published in the *Review*.

or suggestion to his associates, he always publicly accepted the responsibility for any errors or unwise statements in the *Review*. Never once as editor in chief did F. D. N. blame his "young men" publicly, regardless of what loss of points they may have suffered "in the woodshed." His loyalty was absolute and unwavering. He did not make excuses. He courageously accepted the responsibility for the entire *Review*, regardless of whether he was in town or traveling, whether he was intimately involved with the mistake or entirely divorced from it.

What made F. D. N. the kind of man he was? Partly his childhood—the way he was reared.

CHAPTER 3

"Sonny Boy," Child of John and Mary

Young Francis at eighteen months.

THREE little chairs in a semicircle. Three pairs of eyes focused intently on a devout Irish mother and Scotch-Irish father singing hymns. Three piping voices following each song word for word. This was the scene in the Nichol home as John Nichol, father of three little children (a fourth died in infancy), led out in family worship. Dorothy, Mary Jane, and Francis looked forward to worship twice every day, morning and evening. With their bubbling Irish natures, their mother and father made family devotions the high points of the day. "Let's see which of my three darlings can sit quietly for the longest time," Mary would say, and all three would try mightily to win her approbation, the dearest prize of all. This exercise in sitting still served as a learning situation for the little Nichols' participation in Sabbath services.

Thirlmere, New South Wales, Australia, was a long way— half a world away—from the misty shores of the British Isles where both Mary and John Nichol were born, but this devoted couple were living examples of the theory that "while you can take the person out of Ireland, you can't take Ireland out of the person." Warmth, religious fervor, and strong family feeling—these were integral parts of the home into which Francis David was born, on February 14, 1897.

The parents of F. D. Nichol in their younger days.

Irish Mary had been a Catholic, fervent and sincere. Scotch-Irish John had been a Presbyterian, equally staunch. This had caused a bit of conflict. For example, Mary was terribly upset when John refused to permit their first-born child to be christened. She was sure that dear little Mary Jane would be lost as a result. But after their dramatic conversion to Adventism, which came about after finding a rain-soaked copy of the *Review and Herald* along a wooded path, unitedly they dedicated their energies to their new-found, deeply satisfying faith. With typical Irish and Scotch intensity they instilled in the three little Nichols the kind of devotion they themselves felt. They wanted their children not only to love the Lord but to serve their fellow men. Never did they miss an opportunity to instill these values and goals in their little ones.

"We grew up in an age when children were to be seen and not heard," Mary Jane commented recently. "Our parents believed in all the Old World virtues, and they structured our home accordingly."

36

"SONNY BOY," CHILD OF JOHN AND MARY

Mary Fearon Nichol had married John in Australia, when he was supposedly dying of tuberculosis. Doctors had solemnly forecast that he had but three months to live. But John was determined to recover his health. And he did. He lived beyond his "reason of strength" years, to eighty-five.

There were no uncertainties about the future, for if the home was built on anything less than complete security, physically or financially, the children were never aware of it. Mary, strong-minded, vigorous, and John, sparkling, skillful conversationalist, gregarious, very much the "head of the house"— these parents were all that the three children needed to make their world complete. This was fortunate, too, because they

With Nellie Sisley (later Rockwell) as his teacher, F. D. N. began his education in this church school at Wahroonga, Australia.

F. D. N. and his sisters Dorothy and Mary Jane.

37

were all the children had. Every relative was in Ireland or England; the children grew up knowing not a single aunt, uncle, grandfather, grandmother, or cousin. Mary's "landed gentry" parents had disowned her when she married John. So it was that the three little Nichols were molded by the single influence of the home.

Francis and Mary Jane were not far apart in age, so they became "pals" as well as brother and sister. They walked together to school and back each day. On the way through the woods in Wahroonga, they chatted happily about the joys of the day ahead. Once they were startled to find three kangaroos on their accustomed path. Mary Jane felt responsible to protect her little brother, should protection become necessary.

"Oh, don't worry, Mollie," little Francis announced airily. "They're probably going to some kangaroo school of their own!" The wide vocabulary and quick wit were already beginning to show.

The school that the two attended was the first that the Adventists established in connection with the sanitarium work at Wahroonga. It was taught for a time by Nellie Sisley (later Rockwell). The enrollment varied between twelve and fifteen. Five-year-old Francis was the youngest pupil but certainly not the most inconsequential.

One day the teacher was disturbed by considerable tittering in Francis' corner of the room. A number of times she glanced in his direction but each time he looked completely innocent. Not a flicker of emotion showed on his face. When the tittering continued, the teacher called the young pupil to her desk. "Francis," she said, "it seems to me that you're trying to play the monkey this morning. I don't have a cage here to put you in, but rightly I should give you a spat on the hand with this ruler."

Unperturbed, the tiny, mischievous student twinkled, "But, teacher, you wouldn't want to hurt a poor monkey, would you?"

"No, I wouldn't *want* to."

"SONNY BOY," CHILD OF JOHN AND MARY

Quickly Francis offered, "I'll try to be a good *boy*."

"Fine," replied his teacher. "Would you like to sit on my lap for a while?" He would, and did, and that was not the last time he took refuge there.

Small Francis, lively as a cricket, had two brushes with death that could have ended his great potential then and there.

"You must never, never run into the street. You might get hit by a team of horses," his mother, Mary, had cautioned him.

"I won't," he'd assured her.

But one day he forgot and rushed pell-mell into the street —right into the path of a galloping, high-spirited team pulling a wagon.

"Look out! Look out!" bystanders shrieked, expecting and dreading to see a small, mangled body after the horses had passed by.

The driver, though, with frantic jerks on the reins, and bellows of "Whoa, there!" managed to stop the animals just before they trampled the little boy, frozen in his tracks with terror.

Visibly shaken, the driver cursed all small boys soundly and thoroughly. Little Francis was shocked. He'd never heard such language in all his brief life!

A neighbor's cow was the innocent cause of the second near-tragedy. Fascinated by the creature, the little boy loved to climb up on the pasture fence and watch the cow chew her cud or graze peacefully. Once in a while—supreme joy!—he would offer a handful of particularly toothsome grass to her, and she'd obligingly accept it from his hand.

To accomplish this feat, small Francis had to balance carefully on top of the fence—no mean achievement. Neither he nor the cow was entirely sure of the other's intentions. And there were her horns to be considered, enormous and sharp.

Francis became quite proficient in estimating his "lean out" distance. He was proud of this accomplishment; but alas, his downfall (literally) was bound to come. He wasn't sure just

39

how it happened, but there he was, tumbling through the air. Then a sudden, sharp pain under his arm, and gushes of blood. The pointed horn, on which he had landed, had penetrated deeply into his slender little body.

When his mother got him to the Wahroonga Sanitarium for the necessary patching up, the surgeon who treated him looked very grave.

"This boy is fortunate to be alive," he declared, and then went on to describe how death would have been inevitable if the horn had penetrated Francis' body at a point just one inch away.

Mary Nichol offered a fervent prayer of thanksgiving.

In a home where activity was so carefully planned, and where energies were so completely channeled, there was little room for temperament. Fortunately, Francis seldom seemed inclined to manifest any. Blessed with an even disposition, a desire to succeed, and a tractable nature, "Sonny Boy," as his mother referred to him, rarely was in trouble. Not that he wasn't lively. He was. But he was a self-disciplined boy, and this characteristic earned for him the title of "peacemaker" in the home.

John and Mary subscribed wholeheartedly to the "Satan finds mischief for idle hands" type of philosophy. After they moved to the United States, in 1905, when Francis was eight years old, they set about determinedly to see that both they and the children kept busy. Mary had decided to take the nurse's course since they lived close to the sanitarium in Loma Linda. Combining a career and motherhood was a rather revolutionary concept at the time, but with her customary determination she organized the family, giving each member an assignment.

Francis must weed the garden, keep his own room neat, take his turn doing the dishes, and make himself generally helpful. John's work as electrician at the Loma Linda Sanitarium

"SONNY BOY," CHILD OF JOHN AND MARY

(weekly pay $12!) kept him away from the house a great deal of the time, so his home duties were of necessity minimal. Mary had her classwork and studying, besides the cooking and general housekeeping chores. But the three little Nichols were not neglected. Far from it. Worship was still held twice a day, idealism was still talked of and lived, and careful study habits were encouraged.

Elder John A. Burden, whose influence on the Nichol family probably was stronger than anyone else's, and who had brought about their move to the United States, took a deep interest in young Francis.

"How would you like to weed the big vegetable garden near the sanitarium?" he asked the boy one day.

Trained in unfailing politeness, Francis agreed that he would "like it"—although doubtless his typically boyish incli-

The church school at Loma Linda, California, 1906-1907. Young Francis, 9, stands barefoot at right. At the extreme left is his sister Dorothy and behind her his other sister Mary Jane (Mollie).

nations would have preferred some more exciting endeavor. Before long Elder Burden broadened Francis' responsibilities to include helping around the stables. This job, if a bit odoriferous, was also quite satisfying. The well-kept horses, the shiny buggies and carriages, and the opportunity for conversation with the steady stream of visitors delighted gregarious young Francis.

And wonder of wonders, once in a while on Sabbath mornings Elder Burden actually let him drive the horse and buggy to the church at Redlands. This trip of about eight miles was a heady treat! With the reins in his hands, the controlled power of the sleek horses at his command, young Francis David Nichol was in his glory. Perhaps this encouraged him to get started in his next venture.

"Father, may I sell health magazines to the patients at the sanitarium?" asked young F. D. N. one day.

John was surprised—although he learned, as the years went on, never to be surprised at anything his son might attempt to do!

"I'll find out about it, Sonny Boy. I can't see why there'd be any objection to it," he promised.

When arrangements were completed, young Francis worked up quite a clientele for himself, showing the beginnings of the salesmanship that later came in so handy in raising funds for church buildings and increasing the circulation of periodicals. But that was a long way in the future. Young F. D. N. trudged up the hill to the sanitarium, where he canvassed the ambulatory patients with a simple but direct and persuasive speech of this sort:

"I have here a little health magazine that I think you'll find very beneficial. It's a great bargain too. You can't usually buy 'health' for only ten cents!"

Amused by the small boy's play on words, the patients bought the magazines.

"SONNY BOY," CHILD OF JOHN AND MARY

Into the little boy's life came a rare privilege at Loma Linda, one that probably helped to shape his later attitudes. When Mrs. Ellen G. White was a patient in the sanitarium, Francis was introduced to her (probably through the family friendship with Elder Burden). Mrs. White needed to be pushed from place to place in her wheel chair, and Francis, with his two strong, willing little arms, accepted the task with relish. One can visualize the two of them, the then-elderly, feeble, yet keen-minded servant of the Lord, and the small, energetic, bright-faced little Irish-Australian boy who in later life would be one of her strongest defenders.

In her kind way, Mrs. White patted Francis' head one afternoon and told him to be a good boy, and to grow up to be a worker in the Lord's cause. It wasn't a prophecy, only an admonition; but no injunction was ever more dramatically fulfilled. He had been dedicated to the Lord even before he was born. Mary often said that his "heavenly disposition" came as a result of this dedication. And Francis more than fulfilled his mother's—and Mrs. White's—expectations for him.

Mary's years of training in the hospital ended successfully. She passed her examination in the State of California for her R.N. license, so that in the summer of 1910, when the family moved to San Fernando, California, about sixty miles from Loma Linda, she was prepared to augment the income. John continued with his work as a master electrician, while the two older Nichol children were enrolled in San Fernando Academy. The devoted parents, after due deliberation, had come to the conclusion that they simply could not send the three children away to boarding school—they couldn't bear to be separated from them.

Since San Fernando had no hospital in 1910, Mary's Irish ingenuity came up with an idea. Why not run a small maternity home? This worked out beautifully—except for one small problem. Young Francis had to be spoken to very firmly about picking up and fondling the newborn babies! He couldn't resist them. (He never *was* able to resist babies, all the days of his life. Even when wearing a dark-blue suit, he'd pick up a new baby in a fuzzy blanket.)

One thing John and Mary Nichol did *not* believe in was sports. They saw no need for them. They subscribed wholeheartedly to the theory that a young person could get all the exercise he needed by helping out with family duties. "Make every minute count" was an oft-repeated family saying.

One example will suffice to show how this aphorism was implemented. When the family established a greenhouse, young F. D. N. was ordered to pedal home on his bicycle during "vacant periods" (study periods) at the academy to work in it. He was a familiar sight in the little town, pedaling along furiously, brown hair blowing, blue eyes sparkling.

It was not too surprising that young F. D. N. excelled in nearly all fields *except* sports. Having little or no opportunity to develop his muscular skills in this direction, he always made a rather poor showing. A few early experiences seemed to convince him that this just was not his forte.

As he was riding his bicycle one day past the school grounds (on his way to the greenhouse, no doubt) he saw some of his classmates throwing a ball back and forth with what to him seemed consummate skill. Wistfully he alighted from his bike and attempted to join the fun.

"Throw it to me!" he begged. They complied. And he gave a mighty heave with it.

Alas, there must have been a somber fate brooding over young F. D. N. that day. Straight as an arrow the ball soared —right through a window of the church. To have to confess the misdemeanor was serious enough, but to have to confess it to parents who considered ball playing frivolous was twice as serious! Nevertheless, he made amends, and doubtless learned a valuable lesson thereby.

"SONNY BOY," CHILD OF JOHN AND MARY

John and Mary kept their children at their sides whenever possible, so that work could be an opportunity for learning and for "togetherness" (although that rather ungrammatical word hadn't yet been coined). Young F. D. N. worked with his father as an electrician's helper in house after house. At these times he had ample opportunity to observe John's standards of perfection; everything had to be *exactly* right. "Good enough" was a nonexistent phrase for John Nichol. "Exactly right" was how the wiring must be, and the electricians must keep at it until that was achieved. The weary boy could testify that his father never compromised his philosophy.

But the two of them enjoyed each other's company. John's great conversational gift made the time speed by; and his great good humor smoothed over the rough spots that were bound to occur.

In the evenings the whole family gathered in the large house for worship. Worship was followed by study, uninterrupted and serious. The wise parents had placed a large dictionary on a table in one of the rooms, and young F. D. N. soon put it to work. During the day he carried around a pencil and a slip of paper, noting down words that he didn't understand, then in the evening he looked them up. In later years he seldom needed to look up a word. He'd laid the groundwork for his phenomenal vocabulary with the old family dictionary.

Mary and her son had a special closeness that never diminished with the years. She was self-educated in nearly all fields, being a voracious reader. It was definitely not in her plan to be left behind intellectually, even by her gifted son. When he was a man, as the years went on, they'd visit animatedly by the hour whenever they had the opportunity to be together. They'd discuss books, philosophy, theology, and literature—anything and everything. They "operated on the same wave length."

F. D. N. never failed to write to his parents every week, all their lives, after he no longer lived at home. The family ties, created in his youth, continued to exert a strong influence to the end.

Something Mary had said to her son also exerted a strong influence. Over and over, from the time he was a tiny chap, she'd say, with fervor and conviction, "Sonny Boy, you can *amount* to something! You can *be* somebody for the Lord!"

How right she was.

CHAPTER 4

School Life—
Scholarship Mixed
With Fun

AT OLD San Fernando Academy, in California, young F. D. N. achieved high grades. Whatever the scholastic honors available, F. D. N. nearly always earned them. But he was no prig.

Two incidents involving young Francis, both of a non-scholastic nature, have been preserved in the mind of a girl classmate of those faraway days. They leave no room for doubt that he was a prankster, regardless of his high achievements.

The students considered physics an extremely interesting class. Not because of the subject matter but because this was one class in which the boys and girls could work out the experiments *together*. (One wonders if the teachers ever did catch on as to the reason for the splendid dedication shown in this field of endeavor.) Young F. D. N. was already an incurable tease; his famous sense of humor was already apparent.

One day at the old school every time his feminine partner's back was turned, something happened to her experiment—most mysteriously. Feeling quite certain that she knew who the culprit was, before long she caught him red-handed. "Stop it!" she shouted. He piously agreed to desist; but temptation proved too great.

Zetta (his classmate) then picked up a little rubber hammer that they were using in the experiment. Swinging it about

47

her head threateningly, she declared, "If you do anything more to my experiment, I'll hit you with this!"

All was quiet for a moment, then out of the corner of her eye she spied him stealthily moving some of her carefully arranged objects. This was too much. She grabbed the little hammer and swung it at her tormentor. He ducked, but unfortunately, right into the orbit of the hammer. What was intended to be a playful tap turned out to be such a forceful blow that Francis staggered.

Zetta threw down her hammer and grabbed for him. He accepted her steadying hand while his head cleared.

Finally, gingerly massaging his aching head, young F. D. N. weakly protested, "Well, you didn't need to hit me *that* hard."

In later years, when his path crossed Zetta's, he invariably commented that the brisk tap on the head "helped me a lot"!

The physics class apparently had an atmosphere that produced bizarre happenings. On another occasion, when the teacher was absent for the day, the girls hit upon the idea of making fudge while the boys carried on the regular experi-

Francis (left) and Rose (seated) pose with their chemistry class at San Fernando Academy, California, 1914.

ment. With a great deal of merriment it was suggested that the fudge be listed in their experimental notebooks as "No. 23."

All proceeded according to plan. The delicious treat was just ready for "experimental eating" when, with the perverse timing of fate, the teacher returned unexpectedly. There were the students—guilt written all over their faces and the aroma of chocolate hanging heavy in the room.

But young F. D. N. was more than equal to the occasion. With poise and daring befitting a knight, he picked up the fudge, bowed ceremoniously, and offered it to the teacher.

Who could resist such courtliness? Obviously not the teacher. At any rate, no dreadful penalties were invoked. Francis deserved the credit, the class agreed.

Most students consider themselves fortunate if they finish a year's studies with reasonably high grades. In September of 1915, a year and a summer after he had graduated from the academy, young F. D. N. decided that he needed business training. Accordingly, he enrolled in Isaacs Woodbury Business College in Los Angeles, signing up for shorthand, typing, and other related subjects. Imagine the surprise of his teachers when by February of 1916 he had completed the whole year's work, and had mastered the subjects!

Apparently feeling that he still needed to fill in some gaps in his knowledge, F. D. N. enrolled in San Fernando High School the next year, taking subjects that he had not had in the academy. Before long his penchant for the written word, and his talent for producing it, made him a name on the campus. This fact is well documented in *The Orange Blossom*, 1917, the high school yearbook.

World War I was on. The United States had drafted most of its young men, leaving routine tasks to be done by whoever could be pressed into service. To San Fernando High School (and F. D. N.) came the challenge to harvest the beet crop in a nearby valley. The beets must be dug or they would be lost.

4

With patriotic fervor the students volunteered to do the job. They did it successfully. Then on Tuesday, May 15, 1917, the "beet squadders," as they were called, gave a program to commemorate their achievement. A write-up of the assembly program in the school annual states that "Francis Nichol awed us all by his scholarly paper. Some of the little Freshies are still wondering what it was all about."

And no wonder! For already he possessed a large vocabulary and a crisp, incisive way of putting words together. Here is his "famous" treatise:

"Getting Back to Nature—or How We Saved the Beet Crop"

"The usual peace and serenity that pervades our beloved school was somewhat broken into for a couple of weeks this Spring. It appears that a great portion of our valley is planted to sugar beets which need to be thinned out to about one in a foot, in order to allow them to expand to the size natural in our fertile valley. When the time for thinning came this season, thinners were noticeable mostly by their absence, and so the call for help came to us, and out we turned in a body to save the beet crop.

"When we reached the fields a little hoe was given to each of us. On examination it could be seen that this small garden implement had formerly been an ordinary hoe, but by some process, violent or otherwise, it had parted with its handle, at least most of it. The second thing that impressed us was the enormous number of beets that seemed to be able to grow together peaceably in one row, also the great number of rows that one field could contain. With apologies to Tennyson I might say:

> "Beets to the right of us,
> Beets to the left of us,
> Beets in front of us,
> Beets by the hundred.

50

SCHOOL LIFE—SCHOLARSHIP MIXED WITH FUN

"These were the things that impressed us most on first reaching the fields. You may wonder why I dwell on the fact that those hoes were exceedingly short. I will try to explain, for on the size of our hoes depended the *modus operandi* of saving the crop. You see that in order to get at the beets with these implements we had to go on all fours, a method of locomotion which seemed wholly foreign to us, despite the assertions of some of the most learned men of our day that in past ages it was the only method used. By the way, if there is anything in that yarn about evolution, I don't blame our ancestors a bit for rushing through the quadruped stage, for it's a sight easier to travel over the land with one's backbone at right angles to the ground than the old horizontal method. Personally I can't but believe that had Darwin spent the early years of his life on a farm thinning beets the world today would hold a different theory on evolution, at least the part relating to earlier methods of locomotion.

"When the hoes were given us, we were each apportioned four rows to thin, so that there would be only one beet to about every foot. We must not leave more than one, in no case a double. Incidentally we were told that to each acre there were eleven rows and that each row was one-half mile long. I have read of optical illusions, but I believe that that day I saw one, for I could have sworn on my oath that those rows extended halfway to Burbank. If you wish to look upon the longest half mile you ever saw in your life, just go out to the field where we were working and get on your hands and knees at one end of a row and sight along to the other. The effect will be greatly heightened, if you can for the moment let yourself think that you have to go that whole distance on all fours, chopping out beets the meanwhile. You may, dear reader, begin to understand the magnitude of the task that lay before us, and that there was some motive other than monetary remuneration, as an incentive, when we willingly went on a pilgrimage of five

51

Astronomy class under Prof. Wallace Newton at Pacific Union College in 1919. F. D. N. third from right.

Graduation class of 1914, San Fernando Academy. Left rear, F. D. N. Left front, Rose Macklin ("The Golden Girl").

and one-half miles on our hands and knees, to every acre, although the only visible reward was the modest sum of six dollars. Just about enough to pay for having our trousers kept pressed, for somehow they had a tendency to bag at the knees when we went along in that fashion.

"As the days went by, it became noticeable that some were able to cover the ground much faster than others. The reason for this was due to one or more of the following causes. First, strength of the motive impelling; second, kind of soil in the row; third, nearness to primeval ancestors. It did not seem to make much difference to some what angle their backbone made with the earth. Indeed there were a few who were as comfortable when it was measured full length on the ground, though of course that was generally during the noon hour.

"Thus we toiled each day up one row and down another, row after row, day after day. In fact, we might have been going yet had it not been that we ran out of beets. We literally worked ourselves out of a job. Yet during the short time we were in the fields we did the equivalent of a row of beets three hundred miles long. Imagine if you can, a row of beets growing beside the railroad tracks from here up past Fresno, tunnels and bridges of course excluded. Now imagine one boy starting from here, another from Newhall, another from Saugus, and so on up the track past Fresno, each one thinning out the beets in his section up to the next station. Such was the Herculean task which we accomplished in saving the beet crop. Could any motive other than patriotism, and that of the most practical type, have inspired such a deed?

"There is only one question that presents itself in closing. What will be the moral effect on the beets of having the most scholarly inhabitants in our fair valley to give them a start in life? . . . As one dear old lady was saying to me a few days ago, that she thought it very sweet of the boys to go out and save the beets. I agreed, seeing they were sugar beets . . ."

HIS INITIALS WERE F. D. N.

The beets must have made a deep impression on the nineteen-year-old future editor, for he concluded his essay and his oration with three original poems, "Ode to a Beet," "Those Rows to Be," and "The Iron Bound Beet Hoes." None of the three poems is likely to earn him a place in any literary hall of fame!

In the same yearbook another of his poems praising the football coach and a championship football game over Burbank High School, is entitled "To Coach Millen and His Team."

Those closest to him feel that F. D. N. "found himself"—whatever that hackneyed expression means—during this year. Always determined to be at the top in any kind of situation, he apparently now began to realize that literary pursuits offered great satisfactions.

In a family that prized education as highly as did the Nichol family, one would naturally expect that F. D. N. would have made plans to enroll in a Seventh-day Adventist college almost sooner than immediately. He seems, though, to have faced a problem not unknown to many others—one that begins with "m" and ends with "y."

To solve his financial problem, from June of 1917 to January of 1918 he served as secretary to the president of the Southern California Conference, Elder M. M. Hare. His shorthand and other business subjects proved useful indeed. He was enjoying the job—perhaps too much. One day a former classmate from San Fernando days, seeing F. D. N. in the conference office, gave him a verbal jolt. "Francis, what in the world are you doing here? You should be at PUC!"

That did it. F. D. N. was at PUC in January of 1918, ready to start the second semester. Not content to earn credits for only half the school year, he immediately set himself the task of catching up on all the material in all his classes from the beginning of the first semester, back in September. The challenge that apparently delighted him most was Greek. That he ended the year on the honor roll was strictly in the Nichol tradition.

"What in the world does that mean?" was a question fellow students routinely asked him at the table in the old dining room, where seats were strictly assigned to the students. F. D. N. used mealtimes as a sounding board for his ever-expanding vocabulary, to the discomfiture of meal-mates. Thelma Wellman, a student in the academy, once said to him, "Will you please explain that word?"

Calmly, benignly, he gazed on the, to him, little girl.

"Look it up in the dictionary, sister!" was his emphatic order.

"But how can I, if I don't even know how to *spell* it?" was Thelma's rather pitiful response.

Addressing girls and women as "sister" was not the affectation that some considered it to be, nor was it at that time so much a religious term as a holdover from his early Australian boyhood, where "sister" is a term of respect.

The phrase "sanctified common sense" probably best describes F. D. N.'s most unusual characteristic during his college days. That he possessed an active Christian experience there was no doubt; that he was a "goody-goody" there was considerable doubt! He loved a joke too well ever to be a stick-in-the-mud, but still "sanctified common sense" was his guiding principle, as it remained throughout all his life.

Howell Mountain, on which PUC was located, in those days seemed a bit remote from the mainstream of life. The school's founders gloried in this aspect of the college; indeed, this atmosphere was one they hoped to preserve at all cost. Occasionally students wished that it were otherwise, as in the case of Armistice Day, November 11, 1918. For some time throughout the United States there had been false alarms regarding an armistice. Each time the declaration proved premature. Students at PUC were just as interested in this national situation as college students elsewhere, even though their only contact with the outside world was a crystal radio set wired to one of the beds in the boys' dormitory. Possession of the crystal set alone was a fearful "crime"; so much so that the owner's name to this day has been shrouded in mystery. (It definitely was *not* F. D. N.!) This precarious crystal set conveyed the news to the eager occupants of the dormitory that the Armistice was, this time, a reality, not a myth; the news was authentic!

Racing to President C. W. Irwin's office, several of the more impetuous students importuned him to telephone Napa, a small town about twenty miles distant, and verify the good news for himself.

Drawing himself up to his full height and standing securely on his dignity (which was unequaled, except possibly by that of Prof. H. A. Washburn, history teacher), Professor Irwin declined. "Let us get back to our classwork, young men. We shall not interrupt our routine to trace down rumors," he declared firmly, according to the memory of participants at the scene.

Momentarily routed, but not defeated, the small band of "insurgents" retreated to a private corner to plan their strategy.

"People will be celebrating Armistice Day in every corner of the United States. Why should we be the only ones left out?" queried one young man, obviously a type who liked to live dangerously.

"Why, indeed?" chanted the chorus of voices.

Casting about for some dramatic means of celebration in this remote setting, the band of young patriots (?) soon agreed unanimously that a picnic would be appropriate. Not one whit daunted by their previous rout at the hands of the president of the college, they approached him again. But scarcely had they gotten the word "picnic" out of their mouths when Professor Irwin thundered, "There will be no picnic today! Classes will go on as usual!"

Smarting at this flick from the lash of authority, again they withdrew. Very well then, the picnic would proceed *with-*

out faculty support. Food? Well, why not have something new —a foodless picnic? (Necessity is the mother of invention; the food supply was controlled by the dining room and the matron!) To alert the student body, someone would climb up on the roof of the administration building and ring the bell. They shivered deliciously at their own bravery; had anyone ever before dared to touch the bell without authorization?

"Pass the word around among the student body! When they hear the bell, everyone is to go to the picnic grounds!"

During all this excitement F. D. N. had been a fascinated onlooker. As a recognized student leader, it was assumed that he would fall in at the head of the line, or better yet, that he would lend his very considerable powers of persuasion to "the cause." All sorts of emotions were warring on his face as he remained silent for some time. Then, having made up his mind, he spoke, clearly and to the point.

"I can't go on the picnic with you," he announced firmly.

Shocked silence greeted this declaration. Then, an avalanche of protests.

"What do you mean? Do you think the faculty is fair in not allowing a celebration? Don't you want to be patriotic? What's the matter with you?"

F. D. N.—the young F. D. N.—faced his opponents. No one knew better than he that an unpopular stand of this sort could cause him to be disliked for all the rest of his student days at PUC. With the reasoned, reasonable approach that was one of his hallmarks, he set out to explain his position.

"I *do* think the students ought to be allowed a celebration. I *don't* think the faculty's position is the correct one. And I *am* patriotic," he stated quietly. His blue eyes sparkled as he spoke. "But rules are rules. We have all agreed to accept the direction of the faculty. I thoroughly believe in, and can never accept anything other than, the principles of law and order. That's why I can't join in with you. I just can't."

57

He had one final word to say on the subject. "In a Christian school, it seems to me that Christian principles should always prevail, regardless of provocation."

Well, in a fairy story there'd have been no illicit picnic; the students would have been swayed, to the last man, by young F. D. N.'s eloquent speech. But this *isn't* a fairy story; it's true. The students went on with their plans; they rang the bell, they went out to the picnic grounds, and some suffered the consequences. But though F. D. N. didn't participate, in a dim kind of way his fellow students seemed to grasp the fact that he hadn't taken the position he did merely for the sake of being "different"; they seemed to understand that with much of the fiber of his gregarious, fun-loving being he would like to have been right there with the rest of them, yet he had to be true to his convictions, regardless of the cost to himself. So they forgave him for not joining them.

In later years, when the incident would be recounted during nostalgic and "Do you remember when?" sessions with old schoolmates, he never referred to his stand. He always contented himself with a shake of the head and a "Wasn't that something?" remark.

Friday night testimony meetings, a custom of the PUC of that day, often found young F. D. N. a participant, not with high-flown philosophies, but with down-to-earth Christian statements. "He always said something worth listening to," a classmate remarked recently.

He had already begun to acquire a reputation as a writer and scholar. He spent every possible moment on his school work. One can picture him as a kind of Jovian figure on Mount Olympus (or on Mount Howell!) immersed in the great thoughts of the ages. Most of his classmates tended to regard him as something of a bookworm and a philosopher, as well as a potential debater. On the rare occasions when a "march" was held, he'd usually attend, but instead of participating in the endless marching up and down, he'd be off on the side lines, in brilliant and argumentative conversation with anyone either brave enough or foolhardy enough to engage him in verbal jousting.

History classes under Prof. H. A. Washburn, which posed refined torture for many students, were highly stimulating to young F. D. N. Professor Washburn's technique consisted of selecting a student at least once a week, getting him on his feet, and then throwing questions at him as fast and furiously as possible, for at least twenty minutes. To the timid, the uninformed, and the unscholarly, this was the ultimate in suffering. But to F. D. N. it was a battle of wits in which he held his own, and gloried in the holding.

There were other aspects of his interests that developed during the PUC years—his desire to lead, his aversion to sports, his eloquence in speech. And his scholarship remained peerless, enabling him to finish college in two and a half years, as an honor student. During his senior year he taught full time in the history department. He was also a full-time student—and a bridegroom.

As vice-president of the class of 1919 as a junior ministerial student, he is described by these words that appear beside his picture in *The Mountain Echo,* student yearbook:

"Here is our scholar of deep erudition. Give him but leave to bury himself in history."

No one gave him leave to do that. The active, busy world was calling for the services he could render. So, when he graduated from the ministerial course at PUC a year later he, with his bride, entered the work—the Lord's work—to do his part in giving the three angels' messages.

"She was a Phantom of delight
When first she gleamed upon my sight;
A lovely Apparition, sent
To be a moment's ornament. . . .
A perfect Woman, nobly planned,
To warn, to comfort, and command;
And yet a Spirit still, and bright
With something of angelic light."

—WILLIAM WORDSWORTH
"Perfect Woman"

CHAPTER 5

F.D.N. and His "Golden Girl"

Mrs. F. D. Nichol, on Aug. 11, 1949, a wedding anniversary.

F. D. N.'s DESCRIPTION of the beginning of his romance with the only girl in his life was vivid and unvarying.

"She sat there by the window," he was fond of saying, "and the light streaming through her beautiful golden hair dazzled me to such an extent that I was completely blinded to the charms of all other girls!"

"There" was the old San Fernando Academy; "she" was Rose Macklin; and the "golden hair" was in actuality red—a full, deep, true red, though F. D. N. always used the terms "red" and "golden" interchangeably. This penchant for red hair was to follow him all the days of his life. Any red-haired baby was sure to catch his eye. If he was with Mrs. Nichol, he would say, "Look, darling, look at this gorgeous baby! See, it has red hair! Isn't it scrumptious?" Then he'd turn to the baby and say: "You li'l lollipop!" To tiny tots with red hair, he would say, pointing to Mrs. Nichol, "See, my mamma has red hair too."

F. D. N. used to hint slyly that Rose's accustomed seat by the window was more design than accident. She denies the allegation. Whatever the full truth of the matter, his romance with his "golden girl" (she was ever and always that, through all the days of their life together) definitely did not

61

get off to any soaring start in the small academy during the prewar years of 1913 and 1914. If Francis was dazzled by Rose's incandescent hair, Rose was more than a little surprised by Francis' attire. His family had emigrated only a few years before from Australia, and clinging to old, established customs of dress and deportment, they thought it appropriate that Francis should wear "short pants" to school. In a day when no self-respecting boy would have been seen on the street without "knickers," Francis suffered considerable mental anguish, rugged individualist that he was even then. Where the "short pants" were obtained—whether made or bought—remains a mystery.

So the stage was set, with the dignified, golden-haired girl somewhat aloof but inwardly sympathetic with her oddly dressed, brilliant Australian classmate. And true to the aphorism that says "the course of true love seldom runs smoothly," theirs didn't.

Freedom of association between the sexes was virtually unknown in that era when the word *teen-ager* hadn't yet been coined. It was a stringent rule that a boy and a girl must not even *speak* to each other on the school grounds. This in itself would provide a rather formidable impediment unless the young people were adept at sign language!

Then, to complicate the picture further, there were three other problems: Rose's stepmother, who, though she warmly welcomed the young people into her home, was firmly sure that serious romance had best wait until maturity had been reached; a young man from New Mexico who had a prior claim on the affections of the dignified redhead; and a move by Rose from San Fernando to Glendale Sanitarium where she enrolled in the nurse's course.

Not one whit deterred, young F. D. N. also moved to Glendale Sanitarium—as a bellhop. And there the matter rested. From August of 1914 to June of 1915 he worked hard, covering

F. D. N. AND HIS "GOLDEN GIRL"

miles and miles of hospital corridors, rushing here and there on hospital errands—and spending his free time—— With Rose? Not this original young man! He spent his free time with Rose's five roommates, all of whom lived together happily in a little cottage on the grounds. Endlessly, tirelessly, and determinedly, he visited with the roommates, always bringing the conversation around to the subject most vital to him.

"They got rather tired of this," Rose smiles today as she remembers the situation. "After all, eligible young men weren't easy to find. And here he was, one who was eligible and personable—and unavailable!"

He was more than just personable, as early pictures prove. He was definitely handsome!

It was a foregone conclusion that young F. D. N. had his mind made up. Therefore it seemed "written in the stars" that the "golden girl" became his bride on August 11, 1919, in the old San Fernando church. She wore white satin. Not the stiff, heavy satin so much in vogue today, but the soft silk satin of utter femininity, with appliqués of silk lace, and a long veil.

Elder John Burden, lifelong friend of the Nichol family, officiated. And there were bridesmaids and a flower girl and congratulations from a church full of well-wishers. Then Rose, a graduate nurse, and Francis, needing one more year to graduate at Pacific Union College, set off on their honeymoon —a train trip from San Fernando, in southern California, to St. Helena, about four hundred miles north.

Never one to leave anything until the last minute, young F. D. N. had scoured the hilltop of PUC to find a house suitable for his bride. With great pride he had described to her the furnished place he had found, which, if not luxurious, was certainly comfortable. He was sure she would like it. Basking in her admiration of his ability to "provide," the twenty-two-year-old was both crestfallen and humiliated when upon arriving at PUC with his dusty and weary bride he found that the house was occupied—by the owners who had decided to remain at the college after all. There stood the golden girl and the future editor of the *Review and Herald*—little money, no car, no home.

But not for long! Within a few hours the enterprising young man had found another rental property, across "the valley" from the college grounds. And promptly he carried his bride across the threshold.

"He was so loving, so cheerful, so much *fun*. He simply did not know what it was to be downhearted or to wake up in a surly mood. He bounced out of bed bursting with energy, eager for what the new day would bring——" and as she thinks of the little home on the hillside, so long ago and far away, Rose stops for a moment, as though listening to the strains of soft, half-forgotten music.

Fate, it seemed, had decreed that the young couple must keep on the move. The honeymoon cottage proved only a temporary abode. Then there was another move, and finally they settled in a home formerly occupied by her father and stepmother, who had gone on to Walla Walla. There was a slight problem, however, consisting of a goat and a flock of chickens left in the care of the golden girl and the young F. D. N.

Coming in one evening, F. D. N. exploded, "Rose, that pesky goat simply defeats me. I tell you, I can't milk the creature. For some reason known only to herself she will not cooperate. What in the world do you suggest?"

"I'll milk her," Rose promptly responded. "After all, I saw lots of milking done on the ranch in New Mexico when I was a little girl. You're just not doing it correctly," she chided.

"Ridiculous!" was his rejoinder. "You won't have any better luck than I did."

But F. D. N. *could* be wrong, and he was in this case, for almost at once Rose established a fine rapport with Madame

F. D. N. AND HIS "GOLDEN GIRL"

Goat. And F. D. N. conceived a lifelong love for heavy, white goat's-milk cream.

If the goat was subdued rather easily, the chickens were not. With uncanny skill they insisted on laying their eggs all up and down the hillside, in any clump of grass they could find. "Just picture us in the late afternoon," exclaims Rose, "scrambling about on our hands and knees, searching for those eggs!"

But scramble they did, for even a future editor and his red-haired bride had to eat once in a while. "Home grown" eggs were a vital part of the nutritional budget; the magnificent sum of $30 a month that young F. D. N. was receiving for his full-time "substitute" teaching in the history department of the college didn't have much elastic in it. Incidentally, he was also a full-time honor student.

Probably the tranquil pattern of their home life that was to continue all through the years was set during the early months, even with such distractions as an uncooperative goat and fleet-footed chickens. The golden girl, although a fine nurse, stayed in her home. This was her husband's wish. Young F. D. N. had then, and had always, strong convictions as to the role of wife and the role of husband. He saw himself as provider, protector, the knight going out across the drawbridge each day to slay the necessary quota of real and figurative dragons. His wife was to be custodian of the home, reception committee when he returned, and proud receiver of his devotion.

"I love to have a hot meal waiting for me at noon when I come in!" was the way he expressed his gastronomic philosophy. His bride learned quickly that he expected an entree—a non-flesh protein dish—potatoes (always!), a green vegetable, a salad, and a dessert, preferably pie. And, of course, milk, whether goat's or cow's. At night, then, there would be his greatly loved zwieback, fruit, and perhaps a warm drink. From

The Nichol home at Mountain View, California, during their *Signs of the Times* days.

his Irish forebears F. D. N. possibly inherited a taste for hot oatmeal, which remained an unvarying part of his favorite breakfast menu; that, with fruit, toast, and milk. Not a difficult man to cook for—no gourmet here, just a plain, honest appetite for healthful foods.

But what about all the years that followed one another after the honeymoon cottage? There was a baby girl (she *didn't* have red hair, and probably has suffered guilt feelings as a result); there were homes in Vallejo and Mountain View, California, and Takoma Park, Maryland. There were the ever-increasing heavy responsibilities that went with the sense of purpose, the strong dedication that was to characterize young F. D. N., middle-aged F. D. N., and not-so-young-any-more F. D. N. Through it all, there was the strong, steady flame of the relationship between the two—the quiet, self-contained, red-haired wife, and the effervescent, outgoing, energetic husband.

There was tragedy also—not the dramatic, short-lived tragedy which is soon over, although at its beginnings the home tragedy was dramatic enough. The birth of the baby girl,

F. D. N. AND HIS "GOLDEN GIRL"

Virginia, in November, 1920, almost took the life of F. D. N.'s golden girl. For several days it seemed that each breath would be her last.

During this dreadful period when the sword of Damocles was suspended by the merest thread, young F. D. N., then associate pastor of the Vallejo, California, church, gathered the members around him at a special prayer service for his beloved Rose. Never were there more earnest implorings at God's throne. Afterward, F. D. N. rushed home and into the room where the weakened and weary Rose lay.

"How are you, Love?" he inquired. (He almost always called her "Love" instead of the more formal "Rose.")

"Better than when you left to go to the church, dear," was her whispered response.

His eyes lighting up, F. D. N. demanded, "Can you remember exactly what time it was when you began to feel better? I'm sure it was when we were praying for you!"

How like him that was!

When the dramatic encounter with death ended victoriously, the slow, heartbreaking struggle against constant ill-health began. F. D. N.'s golden girl was never fully well again. She didn't complain; she was never known to pity herself. And he didn't complain. Yet it was all bottled up in his heart—this strong, healthy, vigorous man, who was able to move veritable mountains, yet could not give to his beloved wife the priceless gift of health.

Only one time did he show the emotion that was always there. At twilight, at the end of a weary, pain-and-fever-filled day, Rose lay down upon the couch in the living room with a long sigh of resignation. The baby, Virginia, was asleep. F. D. N. quietly put aside the book he was reading and came over to the couch. Wordlessly he knelt beside her, his handsome head against her shoulder, and wept.

Rose, deeply touched, endeavored to comfort him.

"Francis, I'll be better someday. I know it," and she smoothed his brown hair, already sprinkled with gray.

But still he was silent. His emotions were too deep for words, even to one who dealt always in words.

Except when daughter Virginia had problems or wanted to socialize with her parents, life around the Nichol household was hardly characterized by continual conversation. F. D. N., although invariably happy, bouncy, even noisy, felt that he must make every moment count. If conversation served no useful purpose in the years after Virginia married, it should be dispensed with in favor of reading or of just plain analytical thinking. In whatever house the family lived he had a table be-

Elder and Mrs. F. D. Nichol about 1941-1942.

F. D. N. AND HIS "GOLDEN GIRL"

side his chair in the living room. Piled on the table were books and magazines and pamphlets pertaining to whatever his current interest might be. After a light supper he ensconced himself beside the table—and that was that! Attempts to draw him into trivial conversation were practically fruitless. Promptly at nine-thirty he closed his books and conducted family worship. Time spent in sleeping was deplorably wasted, F. D. N. thought. Yet out of consideration for Rose's precarious health, he observed the early bedtime when he was at home.

"Let's always be reading one of the books of the Bible," he had said to his bride soon after their marriage. This custom they always continued, varying the number of chapters as time permitted. Then each person in the family circle prayed aloud. The circle, of course, was never large, but a very *firm* circle nonetheless!

Being of a rather Spartan turn of mind, F. D. N. subjected himself to a hot-and-cold shower each morning. His outcries of shock from the cold water were the regular morning accompaniment to the sound of the merrily cooking oatmeal on the stove and the fragrance of bread toasting in the oven. Then breakfast—but again silence, while F. D. N. sorted out his thoughts for the day and mentally planned his routine. Once in a while, when urged to communicate verbally, he would reply, "But how can I get everything done today if I don't take time to *think?*"

If F. D. N. had an Achilles' heel, possibly it was his inability to cope with simple household repairs. Nothing so filled him with a sense of frustration as his attempts to fix a leaky faucet, a broken window, a swaying step, a loose tile, or a recalcitrant appliance. He confessed himself to be "all thumbs," and in later years solved the matter by calling in repairmen, rather shamefacedly at times, but with an obvious sense of relief and release.

He had a continuing feud, in the several years before his

69

death, with the kitchen stove, which he declared to be particularly diabolical. The stove, he said, seemed to reach up and with deliberate malice turn off its pilot lights whenever it was left alone. It then proceeded to spew gas fumes all around, endangering the life and limb of the householders. No efforts at repair, either amateur or professional, seemed effective.

"Rose," he announced one day, casting a baleful glance at the offending appliance, "get rid of this thing! Buy a new one —sell this for junk—do anything you want—but get a new stove!"

For F. D. N., who practiced economy with both consistency and fervor, this amounted almost to heresy. Open-mouthed, Rose listened, then meekly accepted the assignment.

In due time, all the business details having been attended to, the gleaming new range was installed, much to F. D. N.'s hand-rubbing, eye-twinkling delight. He had vanquished, once and for all, his adversary.

Alas for pride! His victory was short lived. The new stove proved even more adept than its predecessor at turning off pilots. Philosophical in defeat, he solved the problem by turning off the gas at the wall valve whenever he and Rose were to be away on a trip. He grumbled each time; he made dire threats; but turn off the gas he did, faithfully.

On one of their last trips they returned home in the middle of the forenoon. Eager to get to his beloved *Review and Herald* office, F. D. N. was vanishing around the side of the house, unobserved, he thought. But his golden girl, having checked both the stove and his route of escape, called after him, "Francis, if you want dinner ready when you return, you'd better turn on that stove!"

Intercepted in flight, he turned back, hurried to the basement for his wrench, and returned to the kitchen. There ensued a most frustrating scene. The valve, F. D. N. thought, had a will of its own. It fought him in every conceivable way. First

F. D. N. AND HIS "GOLDEN GIRL"

it would not turn—then when it did turn, it went too far, which was just as bad as not turning far enough. In baffled disgust, he squinted up at Rose, exclaiming, "Do you suppose that there's something wrong with *me?* You'd think I'd have enough intelligence to turn on a miserable gas stove!" The last two words were delivered so explosively that even the valve must have been intimidated, for it meekly yielded to his next attempt. F. D. N. marched off the field of battle victorious, if somewhat scarred.

Throughout the years Mrs. Nichol coped alone with domestic problems for long periods of time, since her husband was destined to travel extensively all over the world—more than 300,000 miles by air alone. He prided himself on "traveling light," and worked out a system to achieve this, which was, like everything else he did, efficient. Mrs. Nichol prepared for him a list of "absolute necessities," not filling in the numbers or quantities of these items. He kept this list in his top bureau drawer. Then he swiftly packed for each trip, varying the amounts to suit the length of the trip.

The system worked well. He laid out his possessions on his bed; she put shirts, et cetera, in plastic bags. Presto! the packing was done, the suitcase (sometimes only a brief case) was closed—and he was on his way.

To Rose, F. D. N. wrote a daily letter, filled with news that he thought might especially interest her. If he saw a red-haired child, he described him to her; if he met old friends, he recounted the conversation; if someone told him a clever story, he repeated it.

Fondly, she states that "he took much of his sleeping time to write to me. He never missed a day on any trip he ever took."

And she never missed a day writing to him, telling him about all the little home happenings—the flowers that had bloomed, the canary's new song, the stove's latest antic (!), the grandchildren's amazing feats.

71

F. D. N. holds two little koala bears near Brisbane, Australia, while on his world trip, 1949.

F. D. N. with two New Guinea chiefs on one of his missionary tours.

F. D. N. AND HIS "GOLDEN GIRL"

On trips together in their car there was a strong sense of companionship as they drove the miles to camp meetings or other gatherings. Often F. D. N. would sing; he had been taught so many hymns as a child that he knew literally scores by memory. (This was noted many times by observers who saw that he seldom needed a hymnal.) So they would drive along, F. D. N. lustily singing, "A Mighty Fortress Is Our God," and Rose listening. With the window open, "You could hear him half a mile away," she smiles.

F. D. N. had a strong aversion to restaurant food. Watery vegetables, wilted salads, stale bread, were not for him—that is, if there was any other solution. In her quiet way his golden girl solved this dilemma when they traveled by car together.

"I'd buy little cans of vegetables that could be eaten cold," she explains. "I'd also take along fruit which I'd canned myself, and dates, and nuts, and raisins. Then, when we started out, I'd have a potato salad and maybe some baked beans. We got along very nicely. My husband was much happier this way than trying to find food that suited his palate in restaurants."

On August 11 every year—their wedding anniversary—without fail a florist's delivery truck would pull up in front of the house, and with appropriate ceremony the driver would present Rose with a large basket of flowers. Even when F. D. N. was at camp meetings, which he frequently was, or overseas, the flowers would arrive. His arrangements with the florist were made well in advance. And always, in F. D. N.'s beautiful prose, there'd be a note for Rose's eyes alone.

A reluctant hobby of F. D. N.'s was walking—long walks, shared by Rose, particularly on Sabbath afternoons. He never *liked* walking—the apparent waste of precious time was a serious frustration to him. However, with his usual self-discipline he accepted the necessity that he obtain sufficient exercise. At these times he conversed with his wife eloquently and at great lengths. On spring Sabbaths, when the air was like a caress; on summer Sabbaths, when heat hung over the land like a blanket; on autumn Sabbaths, when the trees were a symphony of color; on winter Sabbaths, when the landscape was mantled in white—the two of them went walking, walking. Rose wouldn't have missed it. He led, she followed, in their physical and spiritual tradition.

And so, F. D. N. and his golden girl walked together through more than forty-six years of life. It was a happy walk, albeit strenuous at times—particularly during the years when Virginia, "Li'l Nip," was growing up.

A recent picture of the second and third generations of the Nichol family. Dr. J. A. and Virginia Nichol Saxon, and children, David, James, Lawrence, and June. Dr. Saxon is a radiologist in the Washington, D.C., area.

74

CHAPTER 6

Father of
"Li'l Nip"

F. D. N. in his young father days, with daughter Virginia.

"LI'L NIP"—daughter Virginia—never received a spanking from her father; at least, she has no recollection of a single instance when F. D. N. felt compelled to back up a command or punish disobedience with physical force. Whether this represented a philosophy on corporal punishment or whether Virginia simply never committed an outrage sufficiently unspeakable to merit "the laying on of hands" no one knows.

Today as she thinks about her father and his dealings with her, Virginia frequently uses the two words "tolerant" and "fair." To her way of thinking, those two words accurately describe him from the very earliest memories of her small childhood until she reached adulthood.

"Remember, though, that daddy traveled a great deal. He simply wasn't home to face and share the trials and tribulations of a growing girl. When there were decisions to be made, mother just had to make them," Virginia says. "It wasn't that he wasn't interested; it was just that a continent or an ocean often separated us at times when there was a crisis of some sort. I got used to doing without him. Both mother and I yielded to the inevitable—we knew daddy belonged to the entire church, not just to us."

"Daddy" became a somewhat Olympian figure to the little

75

F. D. N. with his "Golden Girl" and their one-year-old daughter "Li'l Nip." F. D. N. had only recently joined the editorial staff of the *Signs of the Times*.

girl, an impressive man who came and went, and who filled the house with his vigorous presence, only to leave a silent void when his appointments took him away again. Upon his many returns, he always brought her a little gift—nothing expensive, sometimes only the tiny package of gum or Life Savers distributed by the airline hostess. But the thought behind the gift made the little brown-haired girl feel important and appreciated.

When the family lived in Mountain View, California, apparently F. D. N. undertook to teach Li'l Nip the difference between her right and left hand, it having come to his attention that she hadn't learned this vital bit of physical information. She skated down the sidewalk in front of the house as he stood in the middle of the walk, enthusiastically commanding, "Stick out your left hand, Virginia. Good! Now stick out your right hand——" on and on, until, satisfied that she had learned, he glanced about for a suitable reward.

Ah—the loquat tree just above his head. Promptly he picked a ripe loquat, and with a courtly flourish handed it to the little girl. Then he went back to mowing the lawn, mentally rubbing his hands together in satisfaction. A job well done!

Virginia grew up with the impression that daddy could do just about anything; that he was an expert in anything he chose to engage in. F. D. N. delighted in her admiration and occasionally engaged in a bit of showmanship just for her benefit.

One evening, when she was a small child, he was typing away briskly on a manuscript—one of many that he brought home to work on at night. He was an excellent typist (a holdover from the old business-college days in Los Angeles). Virginia stood watching him, her round blue eyes as big as saucers.

"You type so *good*, Daddy," she praised.

Mightily pleased, he airily responded, "Oh, do you think so, Li'l Nip?" and went on typing, nonchalantly looking all

77

over the room, anywhere and everywhere but at his typewriter.

"Daddy, I just don't see how you can do that!" the child marveled.

"Why, I can do better than that!" F. D. N. boasted. "I can type *with my eyes closed!*"

He proceeded to demonstrate the truth of his claim, while Virginia was struck mute with admiration. He didn't find it necessary to tell his little admirer that any trained typist can do the same. What father would, under similar circumstances!

There was always something of the small child in F. D. N. himself, in his enjoyment to the hilt of any situation in which he found himself. He and Virginia for a short period of time adopted the custom of playing ball in the house. Undoubtedly the period was shortened because of their ill luck in breaking a cherished vase—a wedding gift to Mrs. Nichol.

"My mother actually wept," solemnly states Virginia. "I can see that vase to this day. It was in several shades of brown;

F. D. N. is seen here as first violinist of the orchestra in his academy days.

I think it had some stripes on it. And you know something? My father looked just as guilty as I did when mother came to investigate the crash. For once, he didn't have a word to say."

After a small blue vase—one of a pair that adorned the top of the piano—went the way of the brown vase, the indoor ball games were halted rather abruptly.

Undaunted, F. D. N. brought home a bag of marbles, and proceeded, on the living room floor, to play marbles with Li'l Nip. He didn't set up rules for the game—nothing so formal as that—but the two of them had a fiercely happy, competitive time shooting each other's marbles out of a circle.

Somehow Virginia continued to have feelings of guilt regarding the vases. When she was in her teens, and interested in art, she painted a water color of the matching blue vase—the one that survived. F. D. N., pleased with this artistic attempt, carried the water color to his office and kept it on his desk for many years. Did he, too, suffer from a sense of guilt?

F. D. N. in his younger days had been a rather competent violinist—competent enough, at any rate, to play a solo at his academy graduation. Accordingly, when Virginia had studied piano for a year or so, and was about ten years old, F. D. N. decreed that each night he was home the two of them would enliven a part of the evening with a piano and violin combination.

Virginia shudders even to this day as she recalls the cacophony they produced. "You have to remember that it had been a long time since daddy had even touched his violin. And I—I had only the most meager knowledge of the piano. About the most you can say is that we both tried hard."

Sometimes they didn't reach the end of the musical composition. In fact, when they did, this was an event to be applauded. At times an uninformed listener would have been uncertain that they were even playing the same selection! But there they were, in the soft summer nights and the crisp winter

The Nichol family during their *Signs of the Times* years at Mountain View, California, when their daughter Virginia was six years old.

evenings—the distinguished, apparently forbidding, successful man, and the small, grave, composed little girl, the violinist and the pianist. Just where Mrs. Nichol was is problematical. Pressing business or tender ears may have called her to the most distant part of the house or yard.

Perhaps Virginia's progress on the piano seemed unnecessarily slow to F. D. N. At any rate, he undertook the study of piano himself just about this time, and thumped away at his exercises, making swift strides toward becoming reasonably skillful on the instrument. But the potential pianist had to give way to the peripatetic preacher and energetic editor.

The musical evenings inadvertently gave rise to the one

really serious childhood clash between Virginia and her father. After the pianist and the violinist had exhausted themselves, often all three of the family sang a few hymns. It was understood that everyone sang; they just did, that's all. But with the perversity of childhood, one evening Virginia flatly refused to sing. With lips clamped firmly shut, she just sat, silent as a stone.

Noticing the small rebel, F. D. N. decided that some kind of parental action was called for.

"Stand up and sing the next stanza, Virginia," he commanded firmly.

Virginia stood up, but Virginia *didn't* sing. F. D. N. was reasonable. Virginia was reasonable. But as she remembers the incident, she never did sing. Somehow the clash of wills was resolved without loss of face to either party.

Clashes were few, because Li'l Nip acquired a workable formula at a rather tender age. She simply sized up home situations analytically, then avoided requests that were almost sure to be greeted by a negative response. Being a rather cooperative child, she seems not to have minded this early adjustment to life's realities. What might have happened if F. D. N. had had a red-haired son with traditional matching temperament is anybody's guess.

F. D. N. was always tenderhearted with his little daughter. One Saturday night there was an entertainment to which *everyone* seemed to be going—everyone but the Nichol family. Daddy, mother, and Virginia stood on the front porch, watched the neighbors streaming by, and greeted those they knew.

Suddenly Virginia started to weep brokenheartedly. "I did so want to go to the program!" she sobbed.

Dismayed, F. D. N. glanced back toward the living room where a pile of manuscripts awaited his attention. Then he glanced at the little tear-stained face.

"Well, Mother, I think we could go, don't you?" he inquired quickly.

The tears having been erased as if by magic, to the program they went.

Childhood summers after the family moved to Takoma Park were notable chiefly for the two weeks the Nichol and T. K. Martin families spent at Herald Harbor, Maryland. There, in a large rented cottage, all was sunshine, sand, swimming—and fun. F. D. N. threw himself into the situation with his customary zest, splashing about like a happy porpoise, rowing purposefully from one end of a small lake to the other, inventing water games for the small fry, and generally being the life of the party.

There was one small, almost stagnant pool called the Sulfur Pool, but as the result of a spoonerism by T. K. it was christened by F. D. N. the Pulfur Sool.

"Anybody for the Pulfur Sool?" he'd shout in a stentorian voice. And then all the little feet would come running, for the swimming was good there.

At night Virginia and the two small Martin girls, after being bedded down, sunburned and contented, would hear the voices of the four grownups in the front of the house, in the soft summer darkness. Their world was secure. They drifted off to sleep to the accompaniment of F. D. N.'s pronouncements, not entirely understood, but reassuring just the same.

F. D. N.'s penchant for coining words was usually at its height on automobile trips across the continent. The invented words often became a permanent part of the family vocabulary. One such word came into being when, in the Midwest, from the car window, F. D. N. observed a farmer on a rather noisy tractor.

"Just look at that man *whonking* along!" he exclaimed. To this day in the Nichol family people "whonk" along.

Small girls may regard their daddy as possessed of all

knowledge and all wisdom; adolescent daughters seldom have quite the same attitude. When Virginia became a student at Takoma Academy, at one point she was given an algebra assignment that seemed to her entirely overwhelming. Promptly she took it to F. D. N., who glanced at the problems, paled, and became, for him, rather silent. Fumbling about with this method and that method, he was getting nowhere. Virginia could hide her impatience no longer.

"Oh, just forget it, Daddy! I'll do it myself," she huffed. And that's exactly what she proceeded to do.

In later years F. D. N. admitted to her that his humiliation was almost crushing that night. "But you have to remember, Virginia, that I simply had no *foundation* in algebra," he protested.

While she may have been willing to accept help in algebra, Virginia was proud to a fault regarding her own ability to handle literary subject matter. Never, never did she allow her father to read a composition before she turned it in. In fact, he was lucky if he was allowed to see the composition after it had been graded. "I'm not going to get my grades in English on your work!" she declared.

F. D. N. accepted her rather regal ruling. One day, though, when she had entered college, he came home chuckling, his eyes twinkling. Something was up. He found his daughter already at the supper table.

"Virginia," he remarked innocently, "I met the student who reads papers for your English teacher."

Virginia stopped, her fork in mid-air. "And?" she inquired apprehensively.

"Oh, nothing much," he retorted airily. "She just wanted to know if I edit your compositions before you hand them in!"

"Well, honestly!" Virginia exploded. "Of all the—and to think I won't even let you *see* them. Well!"

Perhaps F. D. N. *should* have seen them, if one that fell

into his hands was at all typical. Virginia had written about her little dog, Trixie. In describing some of Trixie's mannerisms, she said, "Trixie went out and sniffed the morning messages." Enchanted with this skillful imagery, F. D. N. incorporated it as one of the family sayings.

During the days that his daughter was a student at Takoma Academy, F. D. N. always went home for the noon meal, as did Virginia. And for a certain period of time he conceived the idea of reading poetry aloud to his wife and daughter, between forkfuls of potatoes, beans, salad, et cetera. A particular enthusiasm was Henry Wadsworth Longfellow, who had the signal honor of having his poems declaimed, with force and feeling. "The Psalm of Life" seemed ready-made for F. D. N.'s eloquent rendition, Virginia and Mrs. Nichol being the necessary and appreciative audience.

> "Lives of great men all remind us
> We can make our lives sublime,
> And, departing, leave behind us
> Footprints on the sands of time."

Virginia felt that there was little doubt that her father concurred wholeheartedly with the sentiment of this "old faithful."

When Longfellow palled, F. D. N. went through a Milton period, in which *Paradise Lost* was invariably on the menu along with the entree and vegetables.

"He could really get worked up over that," says Virginia. "I suppose the subject matter would naturally interest him more than some other things."

Another mealtime memory of Li'l Nip was her father's fondness for cream—a carry-over from the goat-milking days at Pacific Union College. He loved it on all fruits, on cake, and particularly on pie. But cream was expensive. And those were depression days—the early thirties—with a tight food budget. Nonetheless, through some sleight of hand on the part of the lady of the house, every now and then a small jar of cream would appear on the table, usually at night—at supper. How F. D. N.'s eyes glistened as he contemplated the treat in store. If Mrs. Nichol had baked a pie to go along with the cream, this was gastronomic paradise.

Then the ritual began. A spoon was placed by the cream jar. Daddy "went first." Carefully he measured out one teaspoonful of cream onto his pie.

"That's one, Daddy!" Virginia would exclaim.

Carefully the second spoonful would be scooped up.

"Two!" chirped the little girl.

And she kept a very accurate record, since it was understood that the cream must be shared equally, down to the very last drop. Daddy wasn't exactly selfish about the cream, but none the less Virginia felt that it behooved her to be rather meticulous about her rationing responsibilities.

Cream he may have loved, but F. D. N. always insisted to his family that he had no liking for ice cream. "I just don't care for it," he stated firmly. But whenever the little girl had an ice-cream cone for a treat, F. D. N. couldn't resist "just one bite." If the bite wasn't forthcoming willingly (and is anything guarded more carefully than a child's ice-cream cone?) he had innumerable clever schemes to secure his bite.

"Look over there, Virginia!" he'd exclaim excitedly. Curious, the little girl would look, and in that flash of time—the small bite. This one-bite-of-ice-cream tradition lasted all his life. He was still devising ways to accomplish his little plot when his four grandchildren were long past the baby stage. But eat an entire ice-cream cone, or a dish of ice cream? Never! "I just don't care for ice cream!" Remember?

So far as Virginia can remember, F. D. N. never made any formal attempt to inspire her scholastically. "Not once did my father sit down and tell me that he expected me to achieve good

Mary Jane Nichol and Dorothy (Mrs. Laurence C. Kelly, who predeceased her brother) with F. D. N., strike an informal family pose.

grades. I knew he did, though. He didn't make any fuss over my grades—but I had the feeling that he thought my best would be quite good. He was such a scholar himself, such a perfectionist, it just wouldn't have occurred to him that I'd be an indifferent student."

She wasn't. She was valedictorian of her academy class.

The little girl had been surrounded with books from the time she was born. Books were what made life interesting; books were what people worked with; books were what you occupied your time with; books were valuable.

This ingrained respect for books gave her a most disquieting experience soon after the family moved to Takoma Park, within a few blocks of the Review and Herald Publishing Association. Hearing fire sirens one afternoon, Virginia was horrified to observe great black billows of smoke ascending from the general area of the Review. She raced up the block as fast as her small legs would carry her. Sure enough, her terrible fears were realized; there were fire trucks, and a crowd of people. She must *do* something. Spying a fireman near her, the child panted, "Oh, please, sir, all my daddy's books are up there!"

Virginia wonders now just why she didn't urge the fireman to rescue daddy rather than his books. (She *hopes* daddy was out of town; she can't quite be sure!) As for the fire itself, only a garage or some other peripheral building was involved.

Some men make a hobby of cooking. Not F. D. N. "The only thing he could cook," Virginia declares, "was oatmeal. He would come in at mealtime, sit down graciously, unfold his napkin, and wait for the meal to be served. That's how mother trained him!"

After the meal, no matter how satisfying, nor how complete, he usually went in search of "a little snack," which might be a cooky, or a piece of fruit, or a small piece of candy. Virginia was always a delighted escort on these forays, sharing in the dividends of whatever snack was discovered.

Fatherhood provides splendid and never-ending opportunities for the exercise of patience. F. D. N.'s situation was no exception. In fact, one incident, recalled by several of the principals in the domestic drama, surely deserves a niche in an imaginary Hall of Fame for Fabulous Fathers. It happened when F. D. N. was an associate editor of the *Signs of the Times*.

Mary Jane, one of F. D. N.'s sisters, and her fiancé were spending a week's vacation at the Nichol home in Mountain View. The famous California weather being at its best, the group decided to take a trip to San Francisco.

F. D. N.'s associate, Alonzo L. Baker, was persuaded to go along—probably because he and F. D. N. with their sparkling conversation could provide good entertainment for the guests. In the front seat of the car were Mary Jane and her fiancé; in the back were F. D. N., Mrs. Nichol, and Elder Baker, holding small Virginia Nichol on his lap.

"Li'l Nip," Virginia, becomes Mrs. Jackson A. Saxon, her father, F. D. N., officiating.

For mile after mile the adults ohed and ahed at the lovely peninsula scenery, and exchanged views on a variety of topics. No one, alas, noticed that small Virginia was becoming pale, and after that, slightly green.

And then it happened. With a dreadful retching noise, Virginia threw up all over Elder Baker, all over the upholstery, all over———

Horrified, the suddenly subdued travelers pulled to the side of the road.

"What in the world, Li'l Nip. . . . Your white dress is all stained *pink!*" F. D. N. exclaimed, as Elder Baker attempted to make himself somewhat more socially presentable.

"That's no mystery," said the somewhat shaken young mother. "The raspberries at breakfast—remember?"

Everyone set about the disagreeable and unavoidable cleanup. But the odor was, it seemed, permanent.

Sensing dimly the discomfiture of the adults, little Virginia began to sob.

"Daddy, I'm so sorry!" she wailed.

F. D. N. hugged his damp, sour-smelling little daughter. With his handkerchief he dried her tears.

"Don't cry, Li'l Nip. You couldn't help it. I'm just sorry that your lovely white dress is spoiled."

Not a word of recrimination did he utter; not even a complaint that "our plans have been spoiled." Most fathers would agree that for this feat alone F. D. N. qualified for a medal, or at the very least, a laurel wreath.

Mary Jane's fiancé had the last word, though. As the considerably chastened group got under way again, he delivered a pronouncement that was designed to completely exonerate the still-queasy child.

"Somebody put sugar on the berries last night," he said. "Apparently this combination, added to her breakfast, produced a bad reaction." Whether his premise was right might be debated; but that the result of the food combination (plus the car ride) was bad was beyond debate.

When Virginia grew up, F. D. N. had the pleasure of officiating at her wedding. How he loved weddings! They brought out all the Irish sentimentality of his nature. This wedding, of course, was special—the most special of all, next to his own. As fate wills it, though, sentimentality couldn't get the upper hand; humor took over. At the reception F. D. N. cornered the bride and groom.

"How in the world did you expect me to perform a wedding ceremony with both of you standing there grinning at me?" he demanded irately. And then he grinned himself. As for the two principals, in typical bride and groom fashion they hadn't even been aware that they *were* grinning!

So then Li'l Nip was married (grin and all) and by and by there were four grandchildren—three boys and a little girl, and all of them in F. D. N.'s eyes were most remarkable. Whenever Virginia and her family announced an impending visit at home, F. D. N. would invariably caution Mrs. Nichol to "be sure that all the appliances are in good working order!" He once remarked to me that he was quite certain the washer and dryer operated for all but six hours during a holiday visit! (This was during the diaper stage, of course.)

The very last father and daughter occasion, only a few months before F. D. N.'s death, was a particularly poignant one. Virginia had asked her father to ride with her into the country to look at some property. She and her physician husband were interested in moving out of Takoma Park. It was a beautiful, sunny afternoon in spring—cool, peaceful. As they rode along, from time to time they would pass a small church.

"Let's slow up and look at this one," F. D. N. suggested repeatedly. Upon ascertaining the denomination of the small edifice, he discoursed philosophically upon differences in religion, changes that have come to Protestantism during the past years, and so on. He also commented that the experience of raising up the Hyattsville church (see chapter 8) had been a dream come true. He recalled the building of the beautiful stone church during the depression years, and then he talked about some of the people in the church and the wonderful time he had had with them.

All his wealth of learning and study, as well as his vivid memories, seemed right at his finger tips that afternoon. The two didn't accomplish much in the way of looking for a country property, but what a wonderful afternoon it was! Virginia, though controlled and poised, cannot speak of it without tears.

"He was so gay, so happy, so good-natured, as always. I couldn't know, of course, that this would be the last day daddy and I would ever really have together."

F. D. N. was a good father, in spite of all his many other interests and responsibilities. He had ideals for his daughter. She knew that he had them. "Remember whose daughter you are," he used to tell her when she was small and he wasn't too sure of her potential conduct.

"Remember whose daughter you are" became her slogan through the years. So closely did she identify with F. D. N. that as a child, when asked to identify herself, she lisped, "I'm Elder Nichol's daughter." And as a growing girl she was still "Elder Nichol's daughter." And as a young woman, "Elder Nichol's daughter."

Sometimes, even today, she finds the familiar words springing to her lips. It is a marvelous thing to be—"Elder Nichol's daughter."

"*. . . sole daughter of my house and heart.*"

—Byron, "Childe Harold"

CHAPTER 7

Young Editor at the Pacific Press

THERE HE stood, campaigning for the *Signs of the Times* in front of a small church congregation in the East. Having preached a sermon that extolled the virtues of the *Signs,* and having promised the church members innumerable good things to come in the periodical for the next year, he was ready to take pledges. He stood there with a blackboard marked in squares, ready to ask the members to finance clubs of fifty, or twenty-five, or five—or one hundred. He hoped to fill in all the squares within a few minutes.

F. D. N. had been in this church before. He knew what the Lord was able to accomplish.

"Now who will take a club of twenty-five?" he began in his own brisk, it'll-be-a-success manner.

A timid hand went up near the back of the room.

F. D. N. was pleased. With this good beginning the blackboard should be filled in record time. He looked back toward the woman to thank her. Wasn't her face familiar? Yes, she had pledged twenty-five in previous years.

"Thank you, thank you, my dear sister," he exclaimed. "I remember last year and the year before that that you took a club of twenty-five, and now you're doing it again. I also remember that last year you invited me home to dinner after church, and what a delightful meal you had for me."

Pleased with himself for remembering so much, he went on, "Now, sister, just how do you spell your name?"

From the back of the room came a small, rather cool voice, "I spell it S-M-I-T-H!"

When F. D. N. returned to Mountain View from his promotional trip and told this story on himself in a morning chapel service at the Pacific Press, the two hundred employees could hardly contain themselves. They laughed—and laughed—especially when F. D. N. concluded the story with the wry remark that he *hadn't* received a dinner invitation that day!

F. D. N. loved the promotional aspect of his work with the *Signs of the Times.* He had joined the staff as an assistant editor in 1921. At that time Elder A. O. Tait was editor in chief, and Alonzo L. Baker was associate editor. Elder Baker, a 1916 graduate of Pacific Union College, had returned often to his alma mater to give chapel talks or Sabbath morning sermons during young F. D. N.'s student years. The latter, fascinated by the facile brain and tremendous fluency of Elder Baker, had introduced himself.

Later, when he was pastor in Vallejo, F. D. N. made bold to write an article for the *Signs,* which he submitted, more in hope than certainty that it would be published. But it was a good article—good enough to catch the attention of the chief.

"Do you know anything about Francis Nichol?" Elder Tait asked his associate.

"As a matter of fact, I do," replied Elder Baker. "I've met him several times, at PUC when he was a student; now he's in Vallejo as a pastor-evangelist. He's quite an unusual young man."

And so there wasn't any dreary letter beginning, "Thank you for your article. We appreciate your writing to us, but the article doesn't fit in with our present publication plans." Instead, young F. D. N. was in print—in the March 8, 1921, *Signs of the Times.* The article was submitted as "The Christian Nation," but it appeared as "The Menace of Medieval-ism."

Elder Baker was so pleased with F. D. N.'s first writing at-tempt that he sent him by return mail a brief discussion on the Sabbath submitted by an inquiring subscriber, and asked that he answer it in two articles. F. D. N. agreed to accept the as-signment, replying that "I suppose these articles will be pub-lished in the weekly. Otherwise my second article would follow a month later and I must therefore preface it with a word or so in order to refresh the matter in the readers' minds. [At that time there was a monthly issue of the *Signs* as well as a weekly.] Please let me know regarding this so that I can plan the exter-nal arrangement of the two articles."

His hope that he could encompass the material in two ar-ticles was overly optimistic. When the articles were published there were four, running in consecutive weekly issues from June 21 to July 19, 1921. By that time the initials F. D. N. were appearing also under spicy short discussions of current happenings in the light of Bible prophecy.

That F. D. N. became an editor surprised no one more than F. D. N. himself. From our vantage point, looking back on his brilliant literary accomplishments, it seems altogether incredible that he ever could have considered any other chan-nel of service. Not so in 1921. On April 3 of that year he wrote to Elder Baker:

"Now just a line dealing with a personal matter. Elder J. L. Shaw [General Conference associate secretary] wrote me some weeks ago asking me if I would consider favorably taking up editorial work. I replied that for a vocation I did not desire to follow it. I thought the matter thus ended, but I learn from the conference office that my name is to be considered for such work, at the Spring Council. Being in a place where you know of such things can you tell me whether or not this is so? If this is so I would like to be prepared in advance to meet the powerful arguments and subtle moral suasion that will be used by the General Conference in its efforts to obtain an affirmative response. Surely a man knows best what he is best fitted to do even though others may think differently."

Elder Baker replied promptly, on April 5:

"Now in regard to the question you ask me about your name coming up at the Spring Council for editorial work. Yes, it is coming up there, or has probably by this time. Brother [W. L.] Burgan [General Conference Press Bureau secretary] spoke to Shaw some time ago saying he thought you would make good in editorial lines, and Shaw wrote us for our opinion. Of course, you have been doing good work in the *Signs,* and we knew of your success in getting into print at Vallejo, so we wrote him if you were agreed we would be very happy to have you come to Mountain View for editorial training. Then there were some others who were interested in the matter that helped along the thing.

"We were somewhat disappointed to read your statement that you do not feel that editorial work is the thing that you should take up. Now, of course, you know best, and it would be foolish for a man to try to do anything that he is not enthusiastic about, so we would not try to argue you into any such course.

"But at the same time I would like to tell you that to my mind editorial work is one of the most interesting and fascinating lines that our denomination affords. As you may know during my school years I had my heart set on teaching in one of our colleges and was heartbroken when forced by circumstances to go out into evangelistic field work. After being in that line of work for about a year, I came down here rather unexpectedly and without much of an idea just what editorial work is. However, after three years' experience in this office and knowing what I do both of evangelistic work and teaching work, I can see no comparison between them. Editorial work presents more

96

opportunity for real development than either of those other branches, and then your opportunity for doing good and for reaching the people is greatly enlarged. If you were to follow the evangelistic field you may have audiences of three to five hundred, while in editorial work your audience runs up into the hundreds of thousands. Sister White has said that of all branches of our denominational activity the publishing work is the most important. Of course editorial work is a requisite to publishing work, so therefore you can see our estimate of editorial work. And then we know that long after our ministers are forced to close their mouths our printing presses will go on spreading the truth."

F. D. N. apparently "saw the light," for within a few months he was at the Pacific Press to begin his long, fruitful ministry in the denomination's publishing work. Two years later, on August 18, 1923, he was ordained at Oakland. His ordination certificate was signed by A. G. Daniells, J. L. McElhany, and G. A. Roberts.

It is doubtful that any editorial office ever had two more intellectual, sparkling young editors than Alonzo L. Baker and Francis D. Nichol. The two had offices side by side, and were in almost hourly contact and discussion. Together they decided what topics should be discussed in the *Signs,* and what authors should be chosen. Elder Baker did most of the corresponding to get the material, while F. D. N. took the heavy end of the promotion. Crisscrossing the North American continent, he usually averaged about 25,000 miles a year "selling" the *Signs.*

Both young editors scrutinized carefully every article, whether solicited or unsolicited, and if they felt that they needed further counsel, they went to Elder Tait. The latter, secure in the seasoned wisdom of years, allowed the two young men as free a rein as was possible, undoubtedly realizing that two such soaring spirits would become restless and unhappy if kept too rigidly confined. Many times in later years F. D. N.

7

Dr. A. L. Baker; F. D. Nichol at his *Signs* desk. Their debates in the 1920's with Maynard Shipley of the Science League of America on the teaching of evolution in the public schools brought them national prominence.

The editorial staff of the *Signs* in the 1920's. From the left: Mabel Newton, A. L. Baker, Lester Quade, Edythe Ayres, A. O. Tait, Merton Drake, Ernest Lloyd, Ruby Rick.

voiced his appreciation for this unparalleled opportunity to grow and develop.

At that time there was a good deal of controversy on such matters as the "king of the north," some denominational theologians declaring him to be the Turkish Empire, while others declared him to be the pope of Rome. F. D. N. and Elder Baker were often squarely in the crossfire of theological differences. They felt their youth at these times. They were glad for Elder Tait!

All three editors were exceedingly conscious of the power of the printed word. "White-winged birds" might easily become vultures, and turn and rend a writer when least expected.

There was, of course, the relentless grind of a weekly editorial—a kind of bondage from which F. D. N. was never to be free for the rest of his life. Somewhat typical of F. D. N.'s early editorials* was a short one in the November 20, 1923, issue, entitled "The Hope of a Hopeless World."

" 'The world has seldom, if ever, been closer to hopelessness than now. Different temperaments react in their several ways. Some are indifferent, some cloud their minds with all sorts of forebodings, some turn more closely to business, and many pursue pleasure with an abandon that suggests their incapacity to think of anything else worth while. . . . Now, whenever men find themselves in a desperate situation, nothing so preserves hope and courage as the presence of a commanding personality. Human nature is so made.' Thus speaks the editor of a certain conservative religious quarterly.

"His remarks are correct in every particular. None can deny, and thinking men make no attempt to, that there is something radically wrong with the world. Peace plans have not materialized. Europe cries for stability and prosperity, and is mocked by Bolshevism in Russia, rebellion throughout the

---

* See Appendix N for examples of F. D. N.'s early *Signs* articles.

German Empire, and general economic and financial paralysis over the whole continent. . . .

"Truly, in such a state as this, the presence of a commanding personality is the only way whereby hope and courage can be maintained. But where can such a person be found? Among the statesmen?—No. Among the intellectuals?—No. To whom, then, shall we go for hope and courage?—To Christ, who is able to bring peace and hope to the heart that will receive Him. Though the world may be filled with distress and war, the man who has become acquainted with Christ and communes with Him day by day, will know nothing of fear or perplexity; he will possess a peace that passes all understanding."

Between the two young editors there developed a personal friendship as close and warm as their editorial association. They were "France" and "Lonnie" to each other; to Elder Tait they were "Francis" and "Lonnie." They addressed their editor in chief as "Elder Tait"; but sometimes, affectionately, in private, F. D. N. and others called the latter "Daddy" Tait, a term rather descriptive of the role he played in the triumvirate.

With two such ebullient personalities, with two young men of such firm opinions, the atmosphere was a constant round of discussion, good-natured argument, rebuttal, provings of facts (or disproving!), and stimulating research. But never was there anything ugly or small or mean.

Says Dr. Alonzo Baker: "Francis and I argued much of the time. Each of us was always ready to champion his own views and to defend them. But never in the seven years of our very close association was there ever the slightest acrimony or even sarcasm between us. I admired him and I think this was mutual so far as he was concerned. He was very much of an individual and I could not have submerged him or his ideas even if I had attempted to do so. I respected him and his ideas and valued his independence of thought and judgment; and again, I think this was mutual."

100

YOUNG EDITOR AT THE PACIFIC PRESS

F. D. N., future editor of *Life and Health,* of the *Review and Herald, Present Truth,* and *The SDA Bible Commentary,* was only twenty-four years old when he became assistant editor of the *Signs of the Times.* That he was able to function efficiently is no surprise; his intellectual and spiritual gifts were already decidedly evident. That he was able to show good judgment at such an early age is probably the most remarkable feature of this phase of his life. He simply didn't let himself get into situations which would have caused awkwardness and embarrassment for the members of the Pacific Press staff. With a canny sense of the fitness of things, he stayed well within the realm of the appropriate.

Could he take counsel and direction? Yes, according to Dr. Baker. "France accepted direction and guidance and counsel, but from the general manager of the Pacific Press right on down to the editors, we soon found out that we had better dig up some pretty solid reasons for differing with him if differ we did."

F. D. N. always had confidence in his own views. He didn't formulate them hastily. He thought out his positions and attitudes. He expected others to do the same. With the Scotch-Irish determination inherited from his parents, he set about to put his ideas and viewpoints into operation. Often he succeeded. Sometimes he didn't. He was able, though, to accept defeat gracefully. He didn't sulk, storm, or recriminate; he merely made the necessary accommodation and went on with his work with the constant buoyancy that was such a strong part of his nature.

With the publishing plant itself, he established a close rapport. Young and bouncy, he made himself at home in the various departments, becoming acquainted with all the employees. He knew their names. He knew their troubles. He liked them—and they liked him.

The two young editors didn't confine their activities

101

merely to the editorial ivory tower. Taking as their philosophy the idea that participation in life's battleground gave them more accurate material from which to write, they both became elders in the Mountain View church, where they often preached. Neighboring churches, such as Palo Alto, San Jose, and Oakland, constantly asked for F. D. N. and Elder Baker as speakers.

The Missionary Volunteer Society in Mountain View had two ardent and avid supporters in the two young editors, who entered into all the activities, both spiritual and social, with their usual zest.

The two young couples also belonged to the "younger set" of Pacific Press employees, who got together for an evening several times each year in one another's homes. F. D. N. possessed two distinctions that no one ever was able to take from him: he was always able to drink more punch than anyone else, and he could, from a standing position, jump from the floor into an empty barrel without touching the barrel. Then he could jump out again, not touching the barrel with his hands! Since F. D. N. was no athlete, and found no satisfaction in sports, this accomplishment was all the more surprising.

The other young men in the group practiced endlessly. They made attempt after attempt, only to go down in ignominious defeat with the barrel on top of them. F. D. N. would step up nonchalantly, crouch momentarily, and spring into the barrel. How he was able to do this, no one was ever quite certain.

Although he didn't care for tennis or baseball—actually never played these games—young F. D. N. loved to pitch horseshoes. The necessary coordination between hand and eye in this particular skill afforded him the kind of challenge he most relished. When he had a few minutes to spare he'd head for the horseshoe court to further his skill.

YOUNG EDITOR AT THE PACIFIC PRESS

An eagerly awaited event each year was the annual picnic for all the employees of the Pacific Press, sponsored and financed by the Press. Usually it was held at a nearby location. Few employees had cars, not being affluent enough to afford such luxury. When Golden Gate Park in San Francisco, or some other spot farther away was selected, the Press duly arranged for buses to transport the approximately two hundred employees.

But one glorious year the Pacific Press decided that the picnic should be in Capitola, about forty miles away. It was decided to have the Southern Pacific run a special train from the Pacific Press siding over the Santa Cruz Mountains and through the redwoods to a siding in Capitola. This was an event! No one wanted to miss it; no one *did* miss it! More than five hundred people clambered aboard the train, loaded with food, wraps, and all the impedimenta necessary for a day in the sunshine.

Thinking back on that happy, golden day, Dr. Baker says: "France and I decided—and we had three of the typeroom and pressroom men in on it—that we would get out a special paper for the occasion. There were only five of us in on the deal. It was to be a four-page newspaper entitled *The Kapitola Klaxon*. It, of course, played up the stupendous, earth-shaking event of the Pacific Press chartering a special train and loading all employees, their kith and kin, even to cousins forty-two times removed, aboard the train and roaring through the mountains to the Pacific Ocean.

"Not since Balboa and Cook made their discoveries along the Pacific littoral had anything been so sensational as this. Then we spoofed proofreaders, typesetters, pressmen, and practically everyone else, making fictitious quotes from foremen, heads of departments, et cetera, as to their estimation of this tremendous event and its effect on world history.

"After the train was well on its way, France started in at

103

the head and I at the rear coach, and we came through each coach calling out, 'Read all about the big expedition to the big Pacific Ocean. Get the *Kapitola Klaxon!'* "

The whole trainload of picnickers was, of course, delighted. At succeeding annual picnics the two "newspapermen" were besieged with requests that they put out another edition. They were adamant in their refusal, undoubtedly feeling that their initial triumph would be difficult to surpass.

Both the young editors were harassed by a problem spelled M-O-N-E-Y. Rather, they were harassed by a noticeable lack of this commodity. With two such inventive personalities, it is not surprising that they came up with a colorful idea to remedy their financial embarrassments.

"Do you realize that we are dealing with national and international news every day?" one demanded of the other during a lull in *Signs* responsibilities.

"Certainly," was the prompt reply. "What about it?"

"Why don't we write a syndicated column, commenting on the news, and send it to as many newspapers as possible? We can set up a price by the month——" And they were off!

First, a title: "NEWS AND REVIEWS by Baker and Nichol." That, they decided, was both factual and impressive.

Next, sample columns, which they wrote, rewrote, and polished to perfection. Then, using all their considerable persuasive powers, they talked the local Mountain View weekly into setting up sample columns for them.

Third step—a list from the California Newspaper Guide, dozens of envelopes to be addressed, two willing wives to do the stuffing. Enclosed in the envelope with each column was a mimeographed letter informing the editor of each paper just how much the column would cost him, depending, of course, on his paper's circulation. The two ambitious young men had no intention of revealing the fact that even one newspaper that would subscribe would be a boon!

YOUNG EDITOR AT THE PACIFIC PRESS

Employing again their large and forceful vocabularies, the aspiring columnists pointed out in their letter what a serious loss it would be to each publisher if he did not immediately avail himself of the wisdom, insights, observations, and predictions on the state of mankind and the world at large which would be made by the well-informed columnists.

Alas for their hopes! Not even one editor had the perspicacity to take advantage of this once-in-a-lifetime offer. The two young men, rather crestfallen, philosophized for days on the obtuseness of newspaper editors in general, and the whims of fate in particular. A more pressing problem was their need of cash to pay the local paper for its printing job.

One of the best-remembered and most spectacular episodes of F. D. N.'s life at this time were the debates on evolution that he and Alonzo Baker conducted in San Francisco. During the 1920's the question of whether evolution should be taught in the public schools was being heatedly debated in the United States. This was the decade of the Scopes trial (1925) in Dayton, Tennessee, a trial that pitted William Jennings Bryan against Clarence Darrow.

In California the fundamentalist-evolutionist controversy was raging in the newspapers and in public meetings. Typical of the oratory being used is this extract from an address by Maynard Shipley, presented at a mass meeting November 14, 1924. The meeting was sponsored by the Science League of America, of which Mr. Shipley was president:

"We insist that evolutionary science shall continue to be taught in our schools and colleges, and that theological doctrines shall continue to be excluded from them. The issue is clear-cut. There can be no compromise.

"The Science League of America accepts the fundamentalist challenge. The battle is on! No intelligent man or woman can remain neutral in this fight for protection of our schools against the inroads of Mediaevalism.

"We say to Mr. Bryan: You shall not crucify mankind upon your cross of bigotry; you shall not place your crown of ignorance upon the brow of childhood!"

The two young editors were fundamentalists; they thoroughly believed in fiat creation. And since they were editing a periodical that dealt with issues of this kind, they were better informed than the average on this and other topics involving current events.

The speeches and pronouncements by Mr. Shipley were given almost unlimited newspaper space in San Francisco. Over and over this man ridiculed fundamentalist views on creationism. "Absurd" and "ignorant" were two of his favorite adjectives as he endeavored to advance the cause of evolution.

F. D. N. and Baker read these outpourings with growing annoyance. Truth was being dragged in the dust. No one was speaking up for the other side.

In an editorial published in the *Signs* F. D. N. set forth the significance of evolution as a public question. As a result of this editorial, Mr. Shipley challenged him to a debate on the subject.

Discussing the matter with Elder Baker, F. D. N. suggested that they collaborate in the project. It was agreed; then they went to Elder Tait to get his counsel. Mindful of the dangers, he asked, "Do you boys know enough about the scientific arguments for evolution to be able to refute them?"

The two young editors were honest and forthright. Candidly they replied, "No, we don't know nearly enough right now, but we'll set the debates far enough in the future so we can research the main arguments he [Mr. Shipley] will present, and get facts to counter them with."

The challenge was accepted. The dates were set—Saturday and Sunday nights, June 13 and 14, 1925. And then the two young editors began to wonder if they had "bitten off more than they could chew." There was only one way to go—forward. Actually, with their temperament and enthusiasm, no other alternative would have even been considered.

So F. D. N. and his associate settled down for two months of concentrated, intense study. Buying every book on evolution that they could find, they read them forward and backward, feverishly taking notes—taking notes *on* notes.

They worked separately, devoting every waking moment that wasn't absolutely necessary for the production of the *Signs* to this important and much-publicized project. They prayed. They reread the Bible and the Spirit of Prophecy writings. Both men read and annotated all the books on the list they had compiled together.

When the time drew close for the debates, they sat down together and compared all their findings, all their observations, all their conclusions.

"Now," F. D. N. said, "let's map out our arguments——"

"And," chimed in Alonzo Baker, "our rebuttals, and our summations!"

Both debates were to be held in a large, well-known, centrally located hall—Native Sons' Auditorium, 430 Mason Street, San Francisco. F. D. N. was to be first, opposing the proposition, "Resolved, That the earth and all life upon it are the results of evolution."

The second night Elder Baker would debate the question, "Resolved, That the teaching of evolution should be debarred from tax-supported schools." Each speaker would have one hour for his presentation, then fifteen minutes for rebuttal.

Choosing judges for a debate is always a rather delicate business; they must be acceptable to both sides, must be persons of good reputation, and in this case, of considerable erudition. In conference with their opponent, the three men finally agreed upon a panel suitable to all: The Honorable F. H. Kerrigan, judge of the Federal District Court; The Honorable D. A. Cashin, judge of the Appellate Court; The Honorable

107

HIS INITIALS WERE F. D. N.

T. I. Fitzpatrick, judge of the Superior Court. The chairman was Maurice E. Harrison, dean of the Hastings College of Law.

Mr. Shipley seemed to view the whole enterprise with considerable amusement. Here were two young preachers, products of a small denominational college, holding no degrees of significance from his viewpoint, knowing nothing about science —and they were planning to debate him!

At the first debate Mr. Shipley used part of his hour in giving the audience his choice conclusions regarding his opponents.

Then it was F. D. N.'s turn. In his characteristic crisp way, after he had addressed the judges and the audience, he declared, "I haven't time to discuss personalities nor anyone's competence in the field of evolution, nor are we here for that purpose. Let's get on with the argument and let the judges decide who knows what about the facts."

Calling upon the two months of intense research, his prodigious memory, and his voluminous notes, F. D. N. systematically began demolishing his opponent's stand by advancing one fact after another, one argument after another. His *coup de grâce* consisted of his clever use of "authorities" in the field of evolution who differed decidedly on matters, and who differed radically from the stand presented by his opponent.

Playing one authority in the field of evolution off against others, F. D. N. delightedly led the audience (and the judges) to see beyond dispute that the advocates of evolution were hopelessly divided on important facets of their own theory.

It was almost amusing to watch the rapid change of expression on the face of F. D. N.'s opponent. Where there had been smug complacency, there was now annoyance, surprise, even consternation. Who in the world, he seemed to be thinking to himself, is this young Francis David Nichol? Where did he ever learn to present his arguments so cogently? For that matter, where did he learn so much about evolution?

Floundering, Mr. Shipley soon found himself defending one school of evolution against another, and one evolutionary scientist against another, until it was quite obvious to the judges that he was in total rout.

F. D. N. concluded his case by saying:

"It therefore becomes apparent to the honest seeker for light that the question resolves itself into the most momentous of all questions: Are we going to accept as truth a system of interpretation of natural phenomena whose authority is nothing but human authority, or are we going to retain still our faith in the statements of Holy Writ that in the beginning God created the heavens and the earth? The issues are clear cut and definite; and no one who is sincerely seeking truth, need dally long in deciding which viewpoint he should accept. On all supposed points of proof, the scientist finds that the believer in direct creation has an answer whenever the actual situation is studied with careful thought and logical reasoning. The old truths of the Bible still stand the assaults of the enemies of inspired wisdom; and we need have no fear as to the ultimate triumph of truth; for, as one ardent evolutionist himself spoke more correctly than he realized, 'Truth is mighty, and shall prevail.' "

The judges voted that F. D. N. had won the argument.

Next evening it was Elder Baker's turn. He took the affirmative of the proposition: "Resolved, That the teaching of evolution should be debarred from tax-supported schools." Point by point he built his case, then concluded with an effective summary.

With considerably less sarcasm in his voice and manner than he had displayed the previous evening, Mr. Shipley, the speaker for the negative, began his arguments. The two young "uneducated" preachers had obviously shaken his self-confidence to a marked degree. Virtually confessing defeat in the previous evening's debate, he said, "It would take thousands of volumes to lay before you the evidence for evolution. I was asked to lay it before you in one hour."

Reporting the event later in the *Signs,* Charles E. Weniger, who was present at the debate, wrote: "Although the president of the Science League stated that it would take him about five years to tell all that he knows about evolution, he utterly failed to convince his candid-minded audience that evolution is a scientific fact, or that the theory should be taught in the public schools." Nevertheless, the judges voted that evolution *should* be taught in the public schools.

Elder Baker was disconsolate over this decision, not because he was a poor loser, but because he feared that he had let "the team" down. F. D. N. wouldn't even entertain such an idea.

"Look here, Lonnie," he burst out, "the judges undoubtedly felt that they should hand down a 50-50 decision. The very fact that they awarded one debate to us is a victory for both you and me."

Elder Baker appreciated F. D. N.'s generosity of spirit. The morning headlines in the San Francisco papers convinced him that perhaps they really had won both debates, no matter what the judges said. After all, "Evolution Not True But Should Be Taught in the Public Schools" is pretty strong newspaper fare!

Apparently the debates created some stature for F. D. N. and his fellow editor as apologists for the creationist position. Under a banner headline, "Clash Opens War on Evolution at School Meet," the San Francisco *Daily News* of July 23, 1925, published large pictures of "central figures in the evolutionist-fundamentalist war before the State Board of Education." The two men at the top of the page—one on the right, the other on the left—were the "associate editors of *Signs of the Times,* a Seventh-day Adventist publication."

The editors lost no time in preparing to publicize the debates in the *Signs.* In the July 28, 1925, issue, there appeared a center-spread article entitled "The San Francisco Debates on Evolution," reported by Harold W. Clark and Charles E. Weniger. The article began:

"Popular interest in the subject of evolution was well demonstrated on the evening of June 13, when, for over two hours, crowds of people stood before Native Sons' Hall, San Francisco, filling the sidewalk and part of the street, waiting for the opening of the doors for the first of two debates on evolution between the president of the Science League of America, Dr. Maynard Shipley, and the associate editors of the *Signs of the Times,* Francis D. Nichol and Alonzo L. Baker."

Both debates were reported in depth, then they were put into book form, all the five hours' proceedings. In addition, F. D. N. began a series of articles on the subject of evolution, culled from his exhaustive preparation for the debates. These were published weekly in the *Signs.* The young editors really had their teeth well into the subject of evolution. On the last page of the July 28, 1925, issue, they said: "You have only begun to get into the great question of evolution in this number of the *Signs of the Times.*" Apparently they meant it, for the next year, 1926, they published a book under their joint by-line. Entitled *Creation—Not Evolution,* the book's foreword was written by George McCready Price.

As the fundamentalism versus evolution controversy rolled along, someone suggested that William Jennings Bryan, the hero of the fundamentalists, be invited to Mountain View to lecture in the high school auditorium. It seemed altogether fitting that this orator, who had been drawing large crowds throughout the United States with his lecture "The Rock of Ages or the Age of Rocks" should present his message in the community where the *Signs* was published.

The invitation was extended. And it was accepted!

The visit of this three-time Presidential candidate to Mountain View was a high point not only in the life of F. D. N.

but of his friend and associate editor of the *Signs*. The two young fathers, harassed by the necessity of making their small salaries stretch over seemingly endless needs, were particularly impressed with the fee that Mr. Bryan was able to command for a single lecture—$250! This sum does not seem enormous today, but to the two Adventist ministers, in the mid-1920's, it looked like a fortune.

F. D. N. and Elder Baker could hardly wait to hear the lecture. They planned to sit as close as possible to the speaker —even on the front row, if that could be arranged. But fate had even larger plans for them.

In solemn conclave, the "powers" decided that F. D. N. and Elder Baker—well-informed, sparkling conversationalists —should go to San Francisco, meet Mr. Bryan at the train, escort him to Mountain View, take him to a special banquet at the Pacific Press, and then deliver him safely to the high school.

The great day arrived, and so did Mr. Bryan. The two young editors met him and conveyed him skillfully to his appointments. A large and enthusiastic audience at the high school thundered its approval of the lecture. All in all, it was a great day, a day that provided conversational material for many years.

The seven years that F. D. N. spent at the Pacific Press, first as assistant editor of the *Signs,* then as an associate editor, were growing years, filled with study and consecrated activity. They also were years that deepened his commitment to the work of the Seventh-day Adventist Church. He told "Lonnie" on several occasions when they were discussing their dreams for the future, as young men do, that he hoped someday to fill a position of great responsibility in the denomination. Not because he was vain or ambitious; he simply wanted to be useful, to help mold the policies and activities of the church to which he was dedicated.

YOUNG EDITOR AT THE PACIFIC PRESS

Even as a young man, F. D. N. realized that he had ability. He would have been blind had he not known this. But he wanted one thing only—to make a contribution to the cause.

In 1927 he was offered a peerless opportunity. Elder F. M. Wilcox, editor of the *Review and Herald,* asked him to join the staff as associate editor. He talked over the call with his friend and colleague.

"Lonnie," he said, "I really believe God is opening a door for me for greater usefulness. What better training for service could I ever receive than the experience of working under Elder Wilcox?" The decision was made. He would assume his new duties on January 1, 1928.

Then there was the packing, the arranging, the planning, the farewells, the train tickets for himself, for Rose, for Virginia. There was the three-thousand-mile trip from "sunny California" to the gray, midwinter skies of Takoma Park.

From then on, through his years as an associate and as editor in chief, F. D. N. became more and more "Mr. *Review and Herald.*" But he never forgot his early years on the *Signs,* or any of his old friends. Often when he was in California he visited "Lonnie" in person or by telephone. In the mysterious way that the years have of blending and telescoping together, doubtless they were still young editors together. It was a chapter in their lives that both enjoyed—and relived often in memory.

8

"Dost thou love life? Then do not squander time, for that is the stuff life is made of."

—BENJAMIN FRANKLIN

CHAPTER 8

Turning "Spare" Time Into a Clinic and Church

PRODIGIOUS energy and boundless enthusiasm are usually thought to be characteristics of men (and women) who accomplish more in a lifetime than the average person. F. D. N. could appropriately be used as a case study for this belief. He was always looking for something more to do, some project on which to focus his tireless capacities. Rest? Relax? The words were not even in F. D. N.'s vocabulary.

Having settled his family in Takoma Park at the beginning of 1928, and having spent several months familiarizing himself with his work as associate editor of the *Review*, F. D. N.'s restless, seeking mind began darting about for other lines of endeavor. To sit in comfort in the Review and Herald building, even though engaged in giving the gospel to others through the printed page, struck him as less than an exciting role for a "soldier of the cross." At this juncture a group of ministers approached him, asking that he join them in prayer for "greater evangelism."

Imagine their surprise when their invitation elicited a resounding "No!"

Shocked, one of the group asked for an explanation. F. D. N. was happy to supply it.

"Brethren, I believe in prayer, but I also believe in work. I'll pray for evangelism; but I think we should help answer our prayers by holding an effort."

An evangelistic effort, financed and carried on by the em-

115

F. D. N. at his *Review* desk during his evangelistic labors with the Hyatts-ville church. In the background is his secretary, Eunice Graham.

ployees of the Review—this idea began to take shape in his mind. Before long, he was working up enthusiasm in the plant, dropping a word here and there, presenting his ideas at worship hours. And the plan caught on.

The sum contributed by the staff seems pitifully small in today's world of astronomical figures, yet $300, in 1929, was enough to get a program under way. The total was made up of small contributions; people simply didn't have much money to give. That the Review workers were willing to take on the responsibilities of an evangelistic effort in addition to their financial commitments to their own churches was a tribute to F. D. N.'s persuasive powers.

"He was a born leader," says T. K. Martin, art director of the Review, F. D. N.'s close friend and fellow worker in the effort. T. K. should know, for almost at once F. D. N. enlisted

116

him as his chauffeur. F. D. N. had no car, so T. K. became indispensable.

After studying the Greater Washington area and counseling with the Potomac Conference, the aspiring evangelists decided to hold the effort in Alexandria, Virginia. Handbills were printed (by the Review), a hall was secured, duties were assigned to all helpers, the local church supported the program—and the effort was a success.

Meetings were held weekly, on Sunday nights, with T. K. faithfully chauffeuring the speaker (who announced that his messages would be limited to 35 minutes—and sometimes stuck to his promise!) and giving chalk talks himself, as an artist. Weather notwithstanding, the Review effort went on. When a definite interest developed, F. D. N. and his helpers held Sabbath services. Eventually a group of new members were baptized.

It was with a great deal of satisfaction during the following summer that the "evangelists" reminisced about their work. Probably they were suffused in the rosy glow of euphoria that follows a rather difficult, extracurricular enterprise. Undoubtedly there was a good deal of "now that it's over wasn't it wonderful" kind of feeling.

They were wrong—about it's being over. They didn't know F. D. N.

"Now that we have our evangelistic organization all set up, and have held one effort, it would be a shame to disband," he said, in effect. "Just look at the good spirit the Alexandria effort has engendered here at the Review! There's a feeling of closeness, of fellowship, among us that simply didn't exist prior to the effort. Let's keep it going."

The group really didn't need any urging. They had tasted the joy of working for others; they were used to having a place to go on Sunday nights. The only thing they needed to decide was where they would hold the next effort. In counsel with the Potomac Conference, they decided on Cottage City, Maryland. Modest success resulted from the meetings, despite a rented hall that was apparently unheatable.

The United States by this time was in the grip of the depression. Unemployment, hunger, and despair were spreading. But F. D. N. noted that the Bible truths he was preaching gave new hope to those who faced a miserably uncertain future. And so it was almost a foregone conclusion that there would be a third effort—this time in Hyattsville, Maryland. And this effort led to a significant chapter in the life of F. D. N.

In the autumn of 1931 F. D. N. and his associates rented the Masonic Temple in Hyattsville, a community that had not been especially friendly to Seventh-day Adventists. Laymen who lived in the Hyattsville area pledged their enthusiastic support, and the Potomac Conference provided a Bible worker. All other aspects of the meetings were carried on by personnel from the Review and Herald, with F. D. N. as evangelist and leader of the group.

The Lord blessed, but latent prejudice in the community came to the surface. Ministers on Sunday denounced the meetings that were being held, and advised (almost commanded) their members not to attend. Certain pastors even attempted to revive (or instigate) Sunday-closing laws.

Businessmen, fearing loss of profits if they were forced to close on Sundays, appealed to the Adventists. A theater owner in the Hyattsville area asked for an interview with F. D. N.

"I'm going to be run out of business." He almost wept as he sat in the editor's office. "Won't you help me?"

F. D. N. leaned back in his swivel chair.

"My dear sir, we're not interested in keeping your theater open. Adventists do not attend such places; we consider them deleterious to spiritual life."

Crestfallen, the man began to think he had come to the wrong place for assistance.

118

TURNING "SPARE" TIME INTO A CHURCH

"But," and F. D. N. went on with a great deal of force, "we *are* interested in the rights of every person to worship God as he chooses and to have freedom to conduct his business as is best for him. What is it you want me to do specifically?"

A public hearing had been announced, the man explained, at which a judge would preside, and opinions would be expressed on both sides of the issue. Could Mr. Nichol—would Mr. Nichol—use his eloquence on that occasion?

F. D. N. did more than that. He circulated a petition among the Seventh-day Adventists of the area in opposition to the Sunday law, and went to the hearing, suitably armed. One minister after another arose, denounced "irreligious" persons who desecrated Sunday, and claimed that he was speaking in behalf of "hundreds" of Methodists, Baptists, and other churchgoers. But not one of the ministers proved that he was speaking for anyone but himself. When they were all through, F. D. N. arose, walked to the front of the room, and unrolled the lengthy petition.

"Mr. Chairman, my fellow ministers have claimed to represent many people. I make the same claim—but I shall substantiate my claim by presenting to you this list of people who find the idea of Sunday laws completely opposed to the religious liberty guaranteed by the American Constitution."

With glowing phraseology, careful documentation, and complete subject mastery, F. D. N. presented what amounted to a sermon on religious liberty. He mentioned the persecution which the Baptists had undergone in the early days of the State of Maryland, and used other telling illustrations. So greatly was he blessed in his presentation that the proposal was simply tabled; nothing further was done about it.

The Adventists were much more popular in the community—especially with the business people—after this incident. One of the leading druggists remarked wonderingly, "That was the best speech I've ever heard in my life!"

119

F. D. N. speaking at the groundbreaking ceremonies for the Hyattsville, Maryland, church, June 25, 1938. At his left, seated, F. M. Wilcox, *Review* editor, F. D. N.'s predecessor.

It was a happy moment when on June 25, 1938, the first shovelful of earth was turned for the projected Hyattsville church by F. D. N., whose leadership and evangelistic fervor had made it possible.

TURNING "SPARE" TIME INTO A CHURCH

Good speeches are important, but good actions must follow, as F. D. N. well knew. The meetings were bearing fruit, but in those days the distance from Hyattsville to Takoma Park seemed considerable; new believers should have their own church in their own area. Sabbath services were begun on the first Sabbath in January of 1932, right there in the Masonic Temple where the Sunday night meetings were being held.

There were a few annoyances, however. The hall was used on Friday nights by other groups, whose standards were hardly similar to those of the Adventists. So the evangelistic helpers had their work cut out for them early on Sabbath mornings to sweep out the cigarette stubs and the liquor bottles, mute mementos of Friday night revels.

F. D. N.'s alert mind was already steps and steps ahead. There was the small company of believers who had been baptized as a result of the Cottage City effort; geographically, they weren't far away. Now a new small group would soon be baptized. If some of the members from the large churches in Takoma Park would be willing to transfer their membership to the new group, a new church could be formed.

And so it came to pass. On the first Sabbath in May, 1932, the church was organized, with thirty-seven members from the established Takoma Park churches and ten members from the local area. Three weeks later thirteen converts, the first from the effort to take their stand, were baptized. This brought the membership of the infant church to sixty.

A complete organization was set up, with long-time Adventists serving as officers. T. K. Martin was the elder. Incidentally, by this time F. D. N. was the happy owner of an automobile, so that T. K. was released from his chauffeuring chores. But his new responsibilities with the fledgling church were probably more time-consuming than those of "taxiing" the evangelist.

121

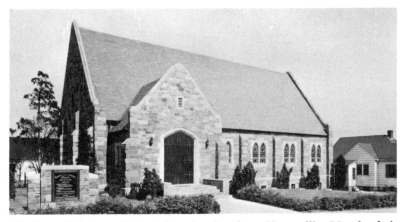

The beautiful Seventh-day Adventist church at Hyattsville, Maryland, is a monument to the evangelistic fervor and consecration of Elder F. D. Nichol. It was dedicated free of debt May 6, 1939.

When one reads a history of already accomplished facts, he gains the impression that a favorable outcome was inevitable; the incidents seem to roll along, one after another, with predetermined smoothness. An excerpt from the official history of the Hyattsville Seventh-day Adventist church illustrates this.

"For seven years the church continued to meet in the Masonic Hall. During that period eighty-three persons were baptized in connection with evangelistic efforts and missionary follow-up with literature and Bible studies.

"During these bleak depression years the church members faithfully contributed to a building fund. To this fund the Review and Herald made a liberal gift. George B. Furman, a prominent Catholic lawyer, who had been favorably impressed by the church's medical clinic, made a gift of one of the two lots secured for a church site. On June 26, 1938, a ground-breaking ceremony was held. The goal was to erect the church free of debt, with the $25,000 raised, even though at the last moment the decision was made to build of stone. To those whose memories run back to the 1930's, it need

The Health Clinic at Hyattsville, an adjunct to the Hyattsville church, and a community service center that won a fine reputation for Adventist welfare work.

hardly be added that $25,000 looked like a huge sum in those grim depression years.

"On the first Sabbath in 1939 the church moved into their beautiful edifice, with all bills paid. The total construction cost, including the seating and other equipment necessary for occupancy, was $24,998.75."

Besides the church, a medical clinic grew out of the Hyattsville effort. The depression, now a grinding, day-by-day reality, had brought into being various kinds of State and county relief agencies, as well as church-sponsored welfare groups. And still there were more destitute and hungry people than could be cared for by existing groups. With the civic spirit that always characterized him, F. D. N. decided that the members of the Hyattsville church should offer their services, both financially and personally, to the local welfare and medical center.

He collected a modest sum of money from his members, took this to the local administrator of the charitable organization, and made arrangements for two women to work at the welfare center. Imagine their surprise when upon arriving at

123

the center they were told politely but firmly that there was no work for them. The atmosphere was cold indeed. An S O S went out to F. D. N., and he responded promptly by paying another visit to the administrator. Hesitantly she informed him that when the local ministerial association had been informed of the financial gift of the Adventists, and of their desire to help, they had threatened to withdraw their support. (The ministers hadn't forgotten F. D. N.'s Sunday law speech!) She was very sorry; but that's how matters stood. And they stood firmly.

This setback obviously called for the laying of new plans. There was so much need everywhere. There was so much to be done. And here were willing workers. Could this small, newly formed church establish a welfare center of its own? Could it operate a clinic? F. D. N. decided to find out. To himself he said, "The Spirit of Prophecy writings say that medical work is one of the most effective means of breaking down prejudice." Someone quoted him as saying wryly that "our enthusiasm for this medical missionary project was exceeded only by our complete ignorance of how to proceed." But proceed they did—with F. D. N. directing implementation of the project.

First, where to set up business. It being depression times, vacant store buildings abounded. F. D. N. and his group reasoned that if a landlord wasn't receiving rent anyway, surely he would be willing to let his property be used for free medical work. This supposition proved correct in the case of Mr. George Furman, who owned a number of vacant stores. Could F. D. N. get the use of one? Surely—the one right next to the County Welfare Agency, which had so summarily declined the help of the Adventists. Poetic justice!

The energetic "do-gooders" swept out the old vacant store, scrubbed it, and washed the windows. F. D. N. asked Bertha Martin (Mrs. T. K.) to assume the position of director—a labor of love—and to wrestle with practical problems, such as obtaining clinic equipment.

On February 21, 1933, the Prince Georges Dispensary and Clinic was opened. In the words of F. D. N.: "We shall give whatever medical aid can be provided by a dispensary, without respect to race, color, or creed." Mrs. Martin's report at the first annual constituency meeting of the clinic tells *how* she wrestled with the problems and how she, and others, solved them.

"Our equipment was very modest. Like the Israelites of old we borrowed, or rather asked outright, of the Gentiles about us, certain furniture, stoves, and the like. And then from our fellow Israelites at the [Washington] sanitarium we obtained an examining table, some disinfectants, and a few instruments. It is remarkable how much can be done with a few secondhand tools and some pieces of scarred furniture."

With wires strung from the ceiling to support green burlap for partitions, the Hyattsville Clinic, as it was first named, was in business! F. D. N., feeling that the agency next door might feel resentful toward the competition, paid yet another call on the administrator. "Since we can't work together, we'll just work shoulder to shoulder with you," he soothed.

At that time there was no hospital in Prince Georges County, Maryland, where Hyattsville was located, and no medical service of the kind that would be offered by the Hyattsville Clinic. The new institution would meet a real need. Therefore, with the cooperation of the local medical society, the Washington Sanitarium provided a doctor on Tuesday afternoons, and the young church provided willing, if inexperienced, helpers. Before long, people from all over the county were coming for help. If they could pay 25 cents, fine; if they couldn't, they were treated anyway.

All went well for a while. Then Mr. Furman obtained renters for his stores. Mrs. Martin, and others, scurried hither and

125

yon to find another empty store. When they found one, they moved in and set up business as usual, until it, too, was rented. For a while they conducted their medical ministry on the stage of the same Masonic hall where they were holding Sabbath meetings. In time Mr. Furman built a small brick edifice on the same block as the new Review and Herald Memorial church and allowed the Prince Georges Health Center, as it was now known, to move in. Dental service was added; the center was open more days each week, and in 1942 the building which now houses the center was finished as its permanent home, next door to the church.

On April 13, 1942, F. D. N. gave his report as president of the board of the Prince Georges Health Center, Inc. In typical style, he constructed his report eloquently:

"At the conclusion of the French Revolution, so distinguished by its anti-clerical outbursts, a noted Catholic abbot was asked as to what he did during the Revolution. 'I survived,' he replied. His answer has become a classic. There are times when it is a sufficient distinction simply to survive. We have thought frequently of this fact in connection with our modest little medical institution known as the Prince Georges Health Center, Inc. Believers in Darwin's doctrine of the survival of the fittest might see in the continued existence of our Health Center an illustration of his survival theory. But we who have been connected with this institution through the years see in its continuing life and growth an illustration of the rational principle of the will to live, combined with the directing hand of a kind Providence. . . .

"As the years passed we gradually enlarged the number and nature of the clinics conducted until today we are busy all week with the exception of Friday and Saturday. The building in which we are so comfortably housed tonight was built without conducting any fund-raising campaign in the county. The whole of the first floor is devoted exclusively to the activities of the Health Center. The floor space is approximately 2,000 square feet and is divided into a large waiting room, a nose and throat room, six medical examining rooms, utility room, nursing supervisor's office, clinic director's office, eye examining room, and two dental offices. . . .

"We have sought to build up an efficient, well-equipped medical center that can care successfully for the physical needs of sufferers. But we have sought with equal earnestness to create an institution that is dominated by a spirit of genuine, gracious charity. We want all who come here to feel that we truly love to help them. We believe we would miss entirely the reason for our existence as an institution if we failed in this. Because we *are* conducting our work in the name of the Great Physician we desire that all who come here shall be warmed and cheered and their pathway lightened by the feeling that the Divine Benefactor of poor mankind has graced this humble place with His benign spirit."

During the time that the Prince Georges Medical Center was drawing its first feeble breaths, and then going on to steady, deep respiration, F. D. N. served as pastor of the newly formed church. In this capacity he was superb. He cultivated that personal touch which means so much to members; he knew every one of them.

One of his practices was that of carrying about with him a church list. On Sabbath mornings, during the announcements or the congregational songs, he would pull out the list, and carefully begin to scan the congregation for absent members. A check mark beside that name. Down the list, another check mark.

His Sabbath afternoon duties were plain to him. He must call on each one, to determine the cause of the absence, and to offer help and encouragement. These visits were in addition to his regular twice-a-year visits in each member's home.

When Sabbath services were first proposed in Hyattsville,

F. D. N. wrote the following letter, dated December 23, 1931:

"DEAR REVIEW AND HERALD FAMILY:

"We hope to begin Sabbath services in Hyattsville the first Sabbath in January. We should therefore proceed at once to organize, so that those chosen to bear responsibilities in the Sabbath school and in the Company may have time to prepare for the first Sabbath meeting. We are therefore calling a meeting at my home, 110 Westmoreland Avenue, for three o'clock next Sabbath afternoon (December 26), for this purpose.

"It is not our desire to stir up a brief excitement and draw a great company to Hyattsville for a few weeks or months. We believe this would not be wise. We hope, instead, for a steady group who will stay. We, personally, are planning to stay there, and, if possible, take part in another Review effort in an adjoining town next winter. Thus we would continue to build up the membership of our Hyattsville Company over quite an extended period of time. Our rent and other incidental expenses will not be heavy.

"Perhaps you feel you have no special talents. Well, your attendance and cooperation in the Company's activities will prove of great value. Or possibly you would like to come, but lack transportation. We believe this can be arranged. Or perhaps you are interested, but cannot yet fully make up your mind. We especially invite you to come to this meeting next Sabbath afternoon, where we can talk over the whole question together. Won't you read prayerfully the enclosed quotations? They may aid you in making a decision.

"Yours for an enlargement of the spiritual activities of the Review and Herald family,

"F. D. NICHOL

"P.S. Don't forget the Saturday and Sunday night lectures at the Hall. Your presence will be a great help."

TURNING "SPARE" TIME INTO A CHURCH

F. D. N. believed in keeping in touch with his members by letter, as well as by personal visits. His pastoral letters were concise, crisp, persuasive, and loving.* Ingathering, church expense, building fund—all the various aspects of church responsibilities elicited from him a letter. These usually were mimeographed. His letter dated November 13, 1935, follows:

"To the Members of the Hyattsville Church

"DEAR FRIEND:

"According to the regular practice in our church we are sending out at this time of the year the ten months' financial statement. Thus the members may know how their account stands with the Lord in the matter of tithe, church expense, and Building Fund, before the end of the year.

"Many of these statements reveal wonderful liberality month by month. God's blessing is upon such liberality. It brings sorrow to our heart, however, when we see some who have been unfaithful to the Lord in the matter of tithe. God's blessing cannot attend such a course. We never really save money by failing to pay to the Lord what belongs to Him.

"Many are faithfully helping to meet the local church expense by regular contributions to this fund. As members of a family we need to share the costs of our church home. . . .

"The Fund for the new church building shows gains. We like to think that every one is planning to meet his full pledge before the end of the year. Or if he has not made a pledge, to give a liberal contribution to this Fund.

"As your pastor I rejoice in the privilege of worshiping with you week by week. May God give to each of you His richest blessing.

"Yours in the Master's service,
"F. D. NICHOL"

---

* See Appendix J for typical F. D. N. letter to a young man from the Hyattsville church who was about to enter national service.

9

On at least one occasion F. D. N. wrote a personal note to each family in the Hyattsville church, apparently typing the letters himself. (The Los Angeles business college hadn't been forgotten!) Each letter was signed personally.

When the church became a wonderful reality, there was the last-minute rush to be ready for the first Sabbath. Members worked right up until sunset on Friday night, sweeping, polishing, carrying out construction debris—all the unavoidable, dirty-hands kinds of things which must be done. F. D. N. was right there, sweeping, carrying, encouraging. One by one, as jobs were finished, the members went home to prepare for the thrilling day ahead. And finally he was left all alone in the church, just as the sun was setting.

He sat down in one of the pews, and gazed around him, at the rosy reflections through the beautiful medallion windows designed by T. K. Martin; at the organ, the pews, the rostrum, the pulpit. And as he realized what God had wrought in the midst of depression with this small group of people his eyes were wet. He bowed his head (even then a clear gray) and breathed a heartfelt prayer of gratitude. His cherished dream of building a church—a beautiful stone church—had come true.

By 1942 F. D. N. found that he could no longer continue as pastor of the Review and Herald Memorial church. In 1933 he had become editor of *Present Truth,* and in 1934 editor of *Life and Health.* These assignments were in addition to his work as one of the editors of the *Review and Herald.* The church by then was a forceful group of people, well able to carry on. F. D. N., as evangelist and then as pastor, had seen to that. But a large segment of his heart never left the Hyattsville project. Many times he declared, "When I'm gone, I'd like to be known as the founder and first pastor of the Review and Herald Memorial church."

CHAPTER 9

The Life and Health *Years*

"THE STRANGE interlude in my life"—that's how F. D. N. always referred to the years during which he was editor of *Life and Health.* He was a minister both by inclination and professional preparation; he had no medical training; but he was a peerless promoter by natural endowment, and an editor always. Therefore, in 1934, when the health journal's monthly circulation dipped to an alarming 26,000, or thereabouts, the Review and Herald board voted to ask F. D. N. to take over. Though he was associate editor of the *Review,* editor of *Present Truth,* builder and pastor of the Review and Herald Memorial church, surely he could find time to devote to *Life and Health!*

Even the dauntless F. D. N. was somewhat taken aback when he was told of the "honor" that had come his way. He arrived home at the regular time, and announced to his wife, "Well, I've just been asked to become managing editor of *Life and Health.*"

Unbelievingly, she asked, *"Life and Health?* Why, medical work isn't your line!"

"You mean it *wasn't* my line until a couple of hours ago, my dear!" And with that, he retired to the back yard, where he sat and thought—and thought and thought. Mrs. Nichol glanced out the window from time to time, but he hadn't moved. He was evolving a plan of action, trying to find some handle to grasp, some place to begin.

F. D. Nichol was editor of *Life and Health* from June, 1934 (shown at top), to March issue, 1946 (below, right). Bottom left is an advertising brochure he published giving facts and figures to help get ads in *Life and Health*. During his editorship the circulation of *Life and Health* went from 26,000 to 260,000 copies monthly.

THE *LIFE AND HEALTH* YEARS

In the June, 1934, issue of *Life and Health* his name appeared as managing editor; then in July of 1936 the masthead carried the line—"Francis D. Nichol, Editor." On the editorial page, which was entitled "The Editors' Comments," F. D. N. published a small editorial with the title "The Best Is Yet to Be"—a title that well expressed his thinking in every phase of life.

"*Life and Health* has completed fifty-one years of uninterrupted publication, and now, as it moves into its fifty-second year, it offers to its readers a larger and still better journal. With this issue we increase the number of pages one third.

"But it is quality as well as quantity that we are endeavoring to give to our readers. Contributors to the journal include a wide circle of nationally known authorities in the medical world. Their presence testifies to the quality of the journal. . . .

"But what makes us even more happy is the fact that the journal has a large and increasing support from laymen— fathers and mothers, business men and women, housewives, children. It is of you we think when we are editing manuscripts for the journal. While we want the doctors to tell you the most scientifically correct things about your health, we want them to tell you such things in a way that you can understand and enjoy, and apply in your own living. . . ."

He went on to state that *Life and Health* had now reached a circulation of about 100,000.

Without question, the most spectacular facet of the *Life and Health* years was F. D. N.'s entry into the world of advertising, for the purpose of operating the magazine "in the black" instead of "in the red." He told T. K. Martin that possibly the hardest thing he ever had to do was learn the advertising trade. The learning was neither accidental nor incidental; he deliberately set about to learn how to solicit advertising from large companies, advertising that would be acceptable for *Life and Health*. He was his own planning committee; he was his own "contact man"; in short, he was his own advertising manager.

Traveling more than 25,000 miles each year in the interests of *Life and Health*, F. D. N. became personally acquainted with key men in the advertising world. He enjoyed visiting big cities such as New York, and seemed perfectly at home with account executives of the large "prestige" agencies. He picked up the "lingo of the trade" with incredible ease; he could talk prices and inches and colors with the best of them.

In order to prime the advertising pump, F. D. N. instructed his office secretary to go through each issue of *Life and Health*, marking all the places that a certain commercial product was mentioned in the articles. It might be whole-wheat cereal, soap, orange juice, a cereal drink—a variety of items. Then the pages were carefully torn from the issues, and these "tear sheets" were sent to the advertising manager of the company which manufactured the product.

"When the man sees that his product is mentioned in our journal, he'll naturally want to advertise with us!" F. D. N. declared triumphantly.

Sometimes it turned out that way. Sometimes not. F. D. N. actually did secure several national accounts, but this wasn't an easy thing to do. Advertising men must spend their money on journals with as large a circulation as possible.

The products that *Life and Health* could endorse were, of course, not too numerous. Then there was the added dilemma of the kind of advertising which the executives would propose. What is acceptable, even desirable, for a secular magazine can be completely *un*acceptable and *un*desirable for a religious health journal. *Life and Health* could hardly publish ads whose appeal depended on bathing suit poses, plunging necklines, and other devices commonly used to sell products. F. D. N. screened the advertisements with infinite care.

His endless work paid off. The circulation climbed steadily

until in 1946 it hit an incredible 260,000—234,000 more than when he came into the editorial chair! This included the circulation of a health journal published by the Pacific Press which merged with *Life and Health*.

But a health journal needs more than advertising. It must have health articles. And F. D. N. had to plan so that it would have those articles. This was an area where he really felt inadequate. Accordingly, he surrounded himself with a great many physicians as consulting editors and as contributing editors. These physicians, among them Robert A. Hare and Charles H. Wolohon, read the galley proofs on all the medical articles that were published. They accepted the responsibility for the authenticity of the positions taken, particularly as related to the Seventh-day Adventist philosophy of health.

F. D. N. meanwhile set about to educate himself in medical lines, much as he had done in advertising, so that he would have at least a grasp of the general scope of the divisions of medicine. Traveling from place to place, he visited Seventh-day Adventist physicians and discussed the health journal with them. Loma Linda, then known as the College of Medical Evangelists, and the first American home he had known, became one of his most frequent stopping places.*

The over-all planning as to what would appear in *Life and Health* went on in the editorial office. One of F. D. N.'s secretaries, Carolyn Eells Keeler, tells it this way:

"We would each keep notes of articles that we thought would be good to have in the journal. Some of the ideas came from the letters to the Family Physician (a question-and-answer column carried on by the physicians who helped with the journal). Some came from articles we saw in other journals. About once every six months we had a meeting to decide upon the articles to write out for."

---

* See Appendix F for comments by Edward R. Annis, M.D., in 1963.

The next step was to procure authors. And here F. D. N.'s carefully cultivated wide acquaintance with the physicians of the denomination paid off. As he went about from church to church, from doctor's office to doctor's office, and to the medical college, he kept careful notes as to who might be capable writers. So then it was merely a matter of assigning, and suggesting a deadline. Quite often it was necessary to extend the deadline, and write gentle reminders, since physicians are unusually busy people.

While at first he wrote few editorials, being content that this matter be handled by the consulting physician editors, as he became more familiar with the medical field, F. D. N. wrote many sprightly editorials, each one bearing his inimitable stamp. In the November issue in 1945, he had compiled what he called "A Picture of Our Subscribers"—and it is pure F. D. N. all the way.

"Would you like to know something about the people who read *Life and Health?* As the result of a questionnaire sent to a cross section of the entire subscription list, we have a rather clear picture of the kind of people who read this distinctive journal. Perhaps you would like to see how near you come to being an average subscriber.

"First of all, 87 per cent of our subscribers are women. That makes sense, seeing that the journal is 'slanted' to that most important group, housewives and mothers. Most of our subscribers are married—93 per cent, to be exact. *Life and Health* makes no foolish claims that subscribing to the journal will enhance one's chances of marriage! We simply give the figures. About 15 per cent of our subscribers are under 26 years of age; 37 per cent are between 26 and 35 years of age; 19 per cent are between 36 and 45 years of age; and 29 per cent are over 45. There is an average of 3.71 persons in each *Life and Health* subscriber's household.

"As to occupations, 80 per cent of the subscribers list themselves as housewives. The average family income is a little under $3,000 per year. Fifty-one per cent own their own homes. The average value of these homes is $4,616.

"And how carefully do they read the journal? This is what really encouraged us. The subscribers could answer the question in one of three ways. And here are their answers: 45 per cent read the journal from cover to cover; 47 per cent read almost every article; 8 per cent read only an occasional article. Then what do they do with the journal when they have finished reading it? They could answer this also in one of three ways. Here are the answers: 24 per cent give it to friends; 72 per cent save it; and 4 per cent discard it. These are figures flattering enough to cheer any editor's heart.

"Because *Life and Health* carries advertising, we also asked a few questions as to subscriber reaction to ads. We reminded our subscribers of the high editorial standards maintained and asked them whether, in the light of this, they had a special confidence in the claims made in the ads. To this question 67 per cent answered Yes, 10 per cent said No, and the remainder expressed no opinion. We asked them also what was the degree of interest with which they read the *Life and Health* ads. They could answer in one of three ways. They replied as follows: 59 per cent read the ads with more interest than those in other journals; 28 per cent, with the same interest; and 1 per cent, with less interest. The remainder expressed no opinion.

"As you read this you can tell where you come in this picture—whether you are an average subscriber or not. We confess we are well pleased with the average subscriber, more than pleased with the better than average—and always hopeful about the remainder.

"No journal could ask for more gratifying responses than those made to our questionnaire by a cross section of subscribers. We are particularly pleased with the response relative to ads. We do not have to tell you that ads are interesting; you know that, and we have a suspicion that you read some of them before you read our editorial page each month! You know that you can depend on what you read in the ads. Now, you are going to see more ads in future issues—not at the expense of articles, no; for there are going to be many more pages to the journal when 1946 begins. But the ads will help to pay for those extra pages that will contain the additional good articles. When you read an ad with interest and have occasion to write to the advertiser, please mention that you read the ad in *Life and Health*. We have not been accepting ads for very long, and naturally advertisers might wonder whether their ads are read.

"By the way, we almost forgot to mention that with paper restrictions removed the printing order on *Life and Health* is now 200,000 per issue. This is by far the largest circulation that any ethical health journal has ever enjoyed. People must really like this journal!"

The copies of *Life and Health* seen in most Seventh-day Adventist physicians' and dentists' offices are not there by accident. F. D. N. pushed this plan. He believed that the best contact patients could make with the denominational health journal was in the office of their family physician or dentist. Since patients who must wait their turn need to be soothed, *Life and Health* has filled a valuable role in this capacity!

During the *Life and Health* era F. D. N. was engaged in researching and writing his book *The Midnight Cry*, thought by many to be his most significant work. Using the early morning hours (3:00 A.M. and onward) for his writing time—his lifelong habit—he usually filled many plastic cylinders with dictation. His secretary would transcribe these the first thing each morning, so that he could read over what he had dictated, make corrections, and be ready for further work. Each cylinder, of course, represented not merely dictation time but careful research. After transcription, each cylinder was "shaved" so that it could be used again.

Upon one occasion, when a new secretary was being trained, three cylinders were on her desk to be transcribed. She typed away furiously, eager to complete the project.

Later, F. D. N. strolled into the office.

"Are the transcriptions ready?" he inquired routinely.

"Surely. Here they are," the new secretary answered, handing him a sheaf of typewritten pages.

F. D. N. riffled through them. "But there should be more. Did you transcribe all three cylinders?"

"Three!" she stammered. "Why, I did only two—Miss [Edna] Edeburn must have done the other one——"

But Miss Edeburn hadn't. And the new secretary, in her understandable zeal to keep the work up to date, had "shaved" all three cylinders.

F. D. N. looked absolutely stricken when he realized what had happened. Many "bosses" would have exploded. Not F. D. N. Realizing that the new secretary was literally frozen with remorse and fear, he merely reassured her that "anyone can make a mistake."

Retiring to his office, F. D. N. closeted himself with the typewritten pages and his dictating machine, and proceeded to repair the damage. Several hours later he emerged smiling and triumphant. The "shaved" cylinder had been redone. And this time the transcription proceeded without tragedy.

The "strange interlude" drew to a close in 1945. Elder F. M. Wilcox retired as editor in chief of the *Review and Herald* in 1944, and a few months later F. D. N. was asked to become his successor. Continuing as editor of *Life and Health* throughout the remainder of the year, his farewell editorial appeared in the April, 1946, issue.

"With this journal we have been associated as editor for the last twelve years. We leave the editorial chair with certain regrets. Journals are like individuals; they have a personality. We are leaving something that has both personality and vitality.

We are leaving a wide circle of loyal and enthusiastic subscribers. We shall miss your letters of commendation—and of
criticism. We have enjoyed them both. We shall miss our fellowship with the circle of brilliant contributors and with the
erudite editorial board. Your contributions and your counsel
have been most valuable."

And so that phase was over. To F. D. N. it may have been a
"strange interlude." To others it was not so strange. They
knew F. D. N. could edit a health journal successfully. And he
had.

CHAPTER 10

Editor of
The SDA Bible
Commentary

F. D. N. surprised by his Commentary associates in Florida motel.

OF ALL THE strenuous years in the life of F. D. N., perhaps the most strenuous were those devoted to producing the *Seventh-day Adventist Bible Commentary*. That F. D. N. and the others who were deeply involved in the project even survived the mountainous task seems proof positive that it was "the Lord's work, and not man's." The magnitude of the project can scarcely be exaggerated.

It began years before in the mind of J. D. Snider, manager of the book department of the Review and Herald. At camp meetings and elsewhere people asked him repeatedly to recommend a "good Bible commentary." The publishing house sold several good ones, but in each case J. D. felt compelled to explain to the purchasers that this part of the interpretation, or that segment of the conclusion, would need to be disregarded, since its theology contradicted the teachings of the Seventh-day Adventist denomination. And it got to be a bit wearying.

"Why," he said to himself, "shouldn't we as Seventh-day Adventists have our own commentary? Why shouldn't we obtain the services of the most competent theologians in our denomination and produce it?"

From talking to himself, it was only one step to talking with others—many others. The idea took root. For those who have never given the matter serious thought, I might point out that a Bible commentary contains not only a book by book,

141

chapter by chapter, verse by verse, comment on everything in the Bible, it also includes many essays on cultural and historical backgrounds. It must be produced painstakingly, accurately, carefully. Decisions must be made, and important judgments rendered. But, of course, someone must do all this. The right human being must be selected as editor.

As so often happened in F. D. N.'s life, the man and the moment and the project met. Those who were getting the idea off the ground asked Francis David Nichol to be editor in chief.

And so he began. He first consulted the faculty members of the Seventh-day Adventist Theological Seminary, located at that time in Takoma Park. From them he obtained the names of students (experienced ministers) who might be of help. He also visited our Seventh-day Adventist colleges, one by one, in order to confer with Bible teachers in these institutions. He wrote scores of letters to ministers in the field, and to other teachers. Those who were interested in helping were asked to indicate the parts of the Bible in which they would prefer to work.

F. D. N. next set out to secure a small permanent staff to scrutinize, organize, and edit the material that would soon flow in from all his "field workers." After a great deal of prayerful thought, careful investigation, and analytical work, F. D. N. decided that the two men he wanted for the undertaking were Raymond F. Cottrell, a Bible teacher at Pacific Union College, and Don Neufeld, Bible teacher at Canadian Union College. F. D. N. was prepared to apply maximum pressure to obtain them. Fortunately, however, both men saw almost instantly that here was a great opportunity to make a lasting contribution to denominational thought. They agreed to become associate editors.

Elder Cottrell and his family moved to Washington in September of 1952, more than a year after F. D. N. had started the initial planning. Elder Neufeld and his family arrived in the spring of 1953. Julia Neuffer, already a research worker at the Review and Herald, was appointed assistant editor.

So there they were, the four permanent members of the staff of the projected *Seventh-day Adventist Bible Commentary*. At first Elder Cottrell and Miss Neuffer shared a small office next to F. D. N.'s on third floor. When Elder Neufeld arrived, all the researchers were placed in a long, narrow room, made by partitioning off part of the third floor chapel (familiarly known as the old chapel). What the setup lacked in glamour and convenience it more than made up in dedication and determination.

From the moment that he agreed to accept the enormous responsibility of being editor and coordinator, F. D. N. began to formulate clear objectives and editorial policies for the Commentary. These are stated in the Preface of Volume I. Briefly, he did not feel that the Commentary should be considered as a final "this settles it" type of theological work.

"The *Seventh-day Adventist Bible Commentary*," he said to his staff repeatedly, "must reflect the best in modern scholarship as well as the various views held by Adventists throughout the years." But emphatically he reiterated over and over, "We are not writing a creed."

Besides establishing guiding principles, F. D. N. set up a time schedule. The schedule was a rather impossible one, but that was the way he did things—aim for the impossible. A volume was to be published every six months; that was the goal. They missed this somewhat, but they made the over-all deadline, to complete the entire seven-volume set in five years. The last volume was published in 1957.

As mentioned, some of the volumes took longer than six months to produce. When the work load got too heavy for the regular staff, F. D. N. would summon from his reserve lists extras who worked for varying periods of time to get the project "over the hump." Earle Hilgert, Alger Johns, Bernard Seton,

143

The SDA Bible Commentary staff: B. E. Seton, Julia Neuffer, D. F. Neufeld, R. F. Cottrell, Leona Running, H. E. Douglass.

F. D. N. and R. F. Cottrell on sun porch working on the SDA Commentary.

Leona Running, and Herbert Douglass were some of the reserve troops who answered the urgent S O S for varying periods of time.

Never one to recommend for others "flowery beds of ease" since he disclaimed for himself an easy program, F. D. N. assured his male co-workers that the "blood, sweat, and tears" of Churchill's war years would seem mild by comparison with the routine upon which they were about to embark. He wasn't just being rhetorical. During those five years the Commentary staff took only one holiday a year, Christmas Day! They worked Sundays, until almost sundown on Friday nights, and often on Saturday nights.

"Elder Cottrell and I very soon got into the habit of trying to be in our office by 4:00 A.M. each morning," Elder Neufeld told me in an interview. "Yet no matter when we arrived, F. D. N.'s office light was shining through his glass door. We'd grit our teeth and actually tiptoe down the hall, hoping to get started so that he would assume we had been there all the time. But before long he would appear in our doorway and boom out, 'Where were you when I arrived this morning?' "

Elder Neufeld smiled as he thought of those dark winter mornings, with snow sifting down, and the soft summer mornings, with sleepy birds calling, and recalled how often F. D. N. would shake his head in pseudo grief and lament, "The thing that saddens me is that today's young men just can't 'take it.' "

Until nearly the last year of the work on the Commentary, F. D. N. kept up this incredible pace. He was, in truth, the pace setter for the rest of the staff.

The picture of himself as a cruel master, driving his slaves before him, amused F. D. N., particularly since the staff was composed of such fiercely dedicated, loyal people. Nonetheless, he took great pleasure in reminding the "sweatshop" associates that he was in possession of the "taskmaster's lash." If, he told them, they didn't produce the tale of bricks he had specified, he would take away their stubble—and *then* where would they be?

Upon one occasion, when F. D. N. was out of the office for several days, his associates decided to arrange a little joke, featuring the "taskmaster's lash." They bought a greeting card which showed the boss's desk unoccupied, and beside it an empty wastebasket. Then they made a little whip by attaching some string to a toothpick. They broke the toothpick in half and taped it to the wastebasket on the card.

F. D. N. accepted the card in good humor—even the not-so-subtle suggestion that he was a "Simon Legree."

Another of his "pet" names for the Commentary staff was "galley slaves," a play on words which delighted him—his penchant for puns was well-known. Dropping into their long, cell-like room before going home in the evening, he was more than likely to peer over the shoulder of one of the men and offer a little speech in this vein:

"Young man, what in the world have you been doing today? When I looked at your desk this morning you were on page 645, and now tonight you're only on page 648!"

He was entirely aware, of course, that his subordinate had spent a long, tiring, and frustrating day wrestling with material that simply would not fall into place properly. He knew what was involved. But this was F. D. N.'s way. And as his associates said of him, "He lived on such a high plane himself, it would never have occurred to him that anyone would be offended by this type of teasing. He was a completely big person. He always assumed that everyone else was too." Most people lived up to this evaluation of them. Without exception his Commentary associates did.

A favorite expression of F. D. N. was that he was a "broker of other men's brains." He had to make the final decision on every line of material that went into the Commentary volumes; he had to be the final authority in matters of theological difference. For him, "the buck stops here" was an awesome reality. It could not be passed any further.

As the material came in from the selected writers in the field, the associates in the office edited, revised, and prepared it for publication, with Miss Neuffer authenticating geographical and chronological areas. Each man often had lengthy conferences with the chief. If the work was not "letter perfect," and a grammatical error or other kind of mistake had been overlooked, F. D. N. pounced on it as gleefully as a cat upon a mouse. He was not overbearing, but his essential and enormous competence had a subduing effect on those around him. Dr. Earle Hilgert is said to have remarked upon one occasion, "When I walk out of F. D. N.'s office after a session with him, I really don't need to open the door. I can just slide under it!"

F. D. N.'s stability in delicate situations, his talent for seeing all sides of a question, and his faith in the efficacy of dialog guided the Bible Commentary safely past many a crisis. As an example, when the material was completed on one of the major books of the New Testament, the galley proofs were sent to a wide range of readers all over the world. F. D. N. and his associates wished to make sure that as wide a consensus of agreement as possible had been reached. In this particular instance the subject matter was definitely controversial, hence an entire segment of readers became exceedingly exercised. An interpretational schism seemed to be looming.

But F. D. N.'s good judgment prevailed. As editor in chief he called together a committee which included the president of the General Conference. Verse by verse, the proposed Bible Commentary material was examined, and verse by verse, the brethren were invited to give their objections. Instead of launching into fruitless arguments, or trying to overpower the dissenters with coercive logic, F. D. N. directed that all the objections be taken down in the minutest detail.

After the committee had gone through this painstaking

F. D. N. cuts his sixtieth birthday cake at a "third floor" party held February 14, 1957. Mrs. Blanche Clymer serves punch as Promise Sherman, F. D. N.'s secretary, assists at left.

F. D. N. is surprised at a special broadcast celebrating his birthday by his Commentary associates.

type of investigation, he and his two associates, with others, spent hours reviewing the apparent conflicts. Could the various viewpoints be brought closer together and be harmonized? F. D. N. thought it possible. And his skillful associates implemented his suggestions by a modification and a synthesis which proved acceptable to all. Again the galleys were sent out. This time, success!

It is fortunate that those engaged in a project as erudite, demanding, and exhausting as that of the Commentary were blessed with a sense of humor. Amusing situations arose. Without them, the enterprise would have been grueling almost beyond endurance.

Probably the most elaborate practical joke of the five years had to do with F. D. N.'s sixtieth birthday. It is difficult to say (or at least no one *will* say!) who originated the idea. R. F. C. wrote a tribute that was simply the ultimate in flowery rhetoric, all of it in praise of that "famous citizen, Francis David Nichol." Elder Dave Olsen, of California, at that time making some recordings at the Review, recorded it. But that was only the beginning.

Elder Neufeld, a clever man with machines, wired a tape recorder so that it would play through the small radio on his desk. He painstakingly recorded the ending of one bona fide radio program, so that when Elder Olsen's voice came on, it would sound entirely authentic, as he announced a program entitled "Washington Celebrities."

Now the stage was set. The plan was to bring F. D. N. onto the scene at the proper time so he would "accidentally" hear the "broadcast." To achieve this, Dr. Siegfried Horn, an adviser whose counsel was frequently sought, was pressed into service. By arrangement, he "dropped in" to the Commentary "cell." A quick telephone call was placed to F. D. N.'s office— "Dr. Horn is here and we'd like to discuss a point with you right away if possible——." Of course the entire third floor had been alerted as to what was about to happen, and the moment F. D. N. disappeared into the Commentary room, everyone clustered outside, suffering from suppressed giggles. The partition surrounding the office space in the old chapel rose only about seven feet toward the high ceiling, so all sounds inside were plainly audible.

Dr. Horn proceeded to raise some involved question, in the midst of which Don Neufeld reached over and switched on his radio, this act eliciting from F. D. N. some rather highly raised eyebrows. His galley slaves listening to the radio while they were working? Now really! He did not, however, make any comment. With his foot, Elder Neufeld then nudged the tape recorder, and just as planned, out of the radio came the words, resonant and professional: "This is Ole Daveson, with your program, Washington Celebrities, the program which brings you interesting facts about famous people in this area . . ."

Not a soul in the room smiled. Their self-control was both amazing and unheard of. The voice went on, "Today we bring you Dr. Francis David Nichol——" and at this, F. D. N.'s head snapped around. Clearly he was suspicious.

"What are you fellows up to?" he asked in dismay.

A chorus of "Sh! Sh!" caused him to subside.

As the incredibly flowery, saccharine speech went on, F. D. N. writhed perceptibly. He kept glancing about the room. But all the faces were composed, tranquil, innocent. Could it be "on the level"? Ridiculous! said his common sense.

At the conclusion of the tape Elder Neufeld reached over and turned off the radio, at the same time clicking off the tape recorder. Then, from outside the room there was a shout of "Happy birthday!" from the third floor personnel who'd been having a real exercise in self-control through all of this. Byron Logan, an art department photographer who "just happened" to have his camera, snapped a picture of F. D. N. before the baffled look faded from his face.

For days afterward F. D. N. tried to "pin down" the situation but no one would admit a thing. Eventually, though, he ferreted it all out. One day he came to R. F. C.'s office and asked for a copy of "the script."

About halfway through the Commentary project F. D. N. had a bout with illness. This indirectly gave rise to another carefully staged practical joke. On order of his physicians, he had been banished to Florida, with strict instructions that he and Mrs. Nichol were to let no one, absolutely no one, know their whereabouts.

"How can you get the rest you simply must have," the medicos asked, "if people from your office are calling you day and night on problems to be solved?"

Since there was no other course of action open to him, F. D. N. took his departure with as much grace as he could muster, mentally looking over his shoulder every mile of the way, and meditating on the volume of work that would pile up in his absence.

It was winter. Takoma Park was in the throes of snow, sleet, gray skies, and all the other spirit-deadening features of the season. As the two associate editors visualized F. D. N. in the land of sunshine, palm trees, blue skies, and balmy breezes, their envy grew.

In this case, as in others, it is difficult to say just when and how the plan began. Probably one day someone remarked idly that "it would be a real surprise to F. D. N. if we should appear down there on his doorstep."

And the response to that suggestion undoubtedly was "Yes, wouldn't it?"

But to the two tired men in the "cell," the mental picture became more and more attractive, until it passed from the "wouldn't he be surprised?" stage to the "I wonder what he'll say—" and then there was left only the implementation.

Elder Merwin Thurber, book editor, happened in on these delightful daydreams one gray afternoon. He was enchanted.

"I'll drive you down!" he offered.

Of course, the three conspirators had the small problem of F. D. N.'s whereabouts. They "thought" that he was "somewhere" in the vicinity of Sarasota; that was enough to start them rolling south—on a Thursday night.

When Friday morning dawned, and the weather became steadily warmer and the sky bluer, the experience was exhilarating beyond words to men who hadn't had a vacation for nearly five years. The two Commentary editors, as a matter of fact, had never been in Florida before; it was a true wonderland to eyes accustomed only to pages of theological discussion, and four walls.

They spent Sabbath in Orlando. No trace of F. D. N. They inquired of everyone, but no one had seen him. He hadn't visited any of his accustomed places. On Sunday morning the men began to feel somewhat crestfallen. They would never regret the trip—but the purpose of it all might never be realized. Then Elder Thurber spoke up, a grin splitting his face from ear to ear.

"I can't keep it any longer," he chuckled. "Last night I telephoned my wife, who'd just received a telephone call from Promise [Sherman]. Are you in luck! Mrs. Nichol had written to Promise on motel stationery. Probably it slipped her mind momentarily that this would be a dead giveaway. Anyway, here we go!"

And go they did, to a Tampa motel. Elder Neufeld had his camera all ready to snap a picture of F. D. N.'s dropped jaw when he opened the door and found his galley slaves free of their chains. But their triumph had to be postponed. The Nichols were out. The carefree editors used their time to good advantage in the surf, however.

When they went back to the motel, their fondest picturizations turned out exactly as they had hoped. They knocked; F. D. N. answered; his jaw dropped; Elder Neufeld snapped a picture; and after a split second of silence, F. D. N. exclaimed weakly, "Well by the beard of the prophet—what in the world are *you* doing here?"

They were invited in, of course, and sat about happily, recounting the history of their little expedition. If they'd entertained any hopes that they'd be urged to stay "for a few days," those hopes were soon dashed. F. D. N.'s chief concern seemed to be over the fact that both editors were traveling home in the same car.

"If you have a serious accident, what will happen to the Commentary?" he fretted.

This horrid prospect put a slight damper on their exuberant spirits. It wasn't long before they excused themselves—and started back home! And so ended one of the shortest sorties into Florida on record. And one of the shortest vacations.

Some time before the Florida trip, the Commentary staff had been wrestling with a particularly difficult portion of the Bible. A consensus could not be obtained for any of the interpretations. The Gordian knot must be cut if it couldn't be untied. F. D. N., a great believer in the efficacy of the outdoors, proposed a weekend campout to clear the cobwebs from the overworked brains. The group would go, he said, to a large cabin on the Appalachian Trail in Pennsylvania. Here there would be no comforts of civilization to detract from the pressing matters at hand. Not even running water.

Arrangements were made, and the staff made the trek, accompanied by the distaff side of each household, as per invitation. After Sabbath morning breakfast, and worship, and study, F. D. N. and the men of the group calmly picked up their chairs and retired to a secluded spot across a small stream, to pursue their theological discussion in tranquil surroundings.

The women, abandoned in this cavalier fashion, staged a small rebellion. "What would they do if we just marched over there with our own chairs?" one feminist is reputed to have asked.

"We'll never know unless we try it!" was their battle cry; and suiting the action to the word, they formed a determined line, chairs in hand.

They said later that F. D. N. really couldn't believe his

eyes, as the feminine contingent simply came, and saw—and apparently conquered. His strong chivalry and innate gallantry triumphed over any dismay he felt. They became a large committee (very large!) for discussion purposes.

In his clever way, though, he put his tormentors to rout. He solemnly asked each wife to give *her* opinion on this complicated matter. And to express an opinion on a deep theological issue, in the presence of experts, is a rather unsettling business. Erelong the women retreated gracefully.

Ever afterward, this weekend in the woods was known by the Commentary staff and associates as the Micheaux Forest Prophetic Conference.

The task that at first had seemed insurmountable finally came to an end. The long, long days—the endless conferences —the writing and rewriting—the little happy and bright whimsical happenings. There was satisfaction in a staggering task well done. But there was a tinge of sadness too. The deep sense of comradeship in the Lord's work which had been developed through all the good days and bad, through all the storms and the sunshine, was a special thing. Now the project that had produced it was complete. The group would be broken up. Each would go on to other assignments.

"We knew that it was a once-in-a-lifetime kind of thing," one of the staff members said nostalgically. "We all felt that we were on a high pinnacle of both interest and usefulness that we would find it difficult to equal again."

F. D. N. was the strong and steady hand at the helm during this, the most ambitious of all his professional undertakings. He was equal to it. More than equal, really, according to his associates.

"I doubt," one of them said, "that anyone else in the Seventh-day Adventist denomination could have done what he did."

CHAPTER 11

The Colorful, Warmhearted Individualist

F. D. N. in 1950, at the age of 53, as he looked when he returned from his second world trip.

THAT F. D. N. was colorful, there is no doubt. His color stemmed partly from the fact that in an age of conformity, he dared to be a nonconformist; he actually seemed to glory in nonconformity. Not for him the cowardly beige of the organization man. He was all in technicolor. In journalistic terminology, F. D. N. was good copy.

Some people make news whenever they open their mouths to speak. F. D. N. belonged to this breed. But even if his statements sometimes were not news, they were entertaining. His gift for repartee was unsurpassed, and he left the other person, or the group, either speechless or red-faced. This delighted him, not because he enjoyed observing the discomfiture of others, but because he reveled in the challenge of "topping" every remark.

One of the classic examples of this phase of his nature was a verbal encounter he had with a representative of the Pacific Press. The incident had to do with a painful year in which the *Review and Herald* published incorrect dates for the Week of Prayer—an error of the first magnitude. Already smarting over the faux pas, F. D. N. winced visibly when the Pacific Press representative gleefully pointed out the appalling mistake in the presence of a large number of people.

155

F. D. N. concentrated for a moment, then rising to his feet and pointing his long, emphatic forefinger at his tormentor, he announced, "All of us carry around with us little books in our breast pockets, published by the Pacific Press Publishing Association. We record our appointments and our plans in them. Brethren, we *rely* on these little books, which contain the daily calendar for the year."

Then, pausing to secure maximum dramatic effect—although everyone seemed to sense what was about to come— he fired his deadly salvo.

"From this little treasure of a book we took the dates for the Week of Prayer. We didn't check further. That, brethren, was our mistake!"

F. D. N. was as individualistic in his dress as in his humor. In later years, particularly, he defied convention if it suited his fancy. For example, when he decided that he needed special attire to keep him warm in winter on his four-mile walk each day to and from the Review offices, he acquired for himself a muted-plaid winter jacket and a "Russian hat." He wore both doggedly, and with considerable relish. He seemed not to mind that fellow workers driving on Carroll Avenue (the home-to-Review route) smiled with amusement as they spotted the brilliant, suave editor "traveling incognito." The question, What will people think? apparently never even occurred to him. If it did, he dismissed it with, "Let them think what they will."

In the past several years beards have become somewhat fashionable, at least with the younger set. This was not the case when F. D. N. made his trips overseas. Beards at that time —particularly in the United States—were unusual, complete conversation-stoppers. But arguing that people in some countries give greater deference to a man with a beard, he set himself the task of growing a full, luxuriant, flowing beard in the several months of his absence.

Opinions differ as to why he grew his beard. On the first

On his trip around the world in 1959 F. D. N. spent about three weeks in the Trans-Africa Division. At that time Robert H. Pierson (background) was division president. Here F. D. N. wears a beard. His right ankle, broken in an accident in England, is in a cast.

trip it is likely that the accomplishment was not the outgrowth of individualism, but the result of a luggage difficulty. He arrived at his first destination sans his luggage. Europe was still suffering intensely from World War II. Certain consumer goods, including razors and blades, were simply unavailable. At least, F. D. N. couldn't obtain them, determined man that he was! His luggage did not catch up with him for two weeks; by that time he was well on the way to a bearded state. Feeling that it would be a shame to waste his endeavors, since beards were highly respected in some countries he would visit, he launched his first hirsute growth.

Those of us who knew him well felt certain that he would descend from his last plane in Washington wearing a snow-white, silky beard, and attracting the gaze of everyone in the airport. We were not disappointed. But Mrs. Nichol was. She gave F. D. N. a deadline, by which time the flourishing beard must go. And go it did—until the next round-the-world trip.

On his daily walks to and from his office—walks that he considered essential to health—he often was besieged by would-be good Samaritans. Persons who didn't know him and his habits, quite often stopped and graciously invited him to ride with them, presuming that perhaps his own car was in the garage for repairs. With a forceful wave of his hand, he usually sent them on their way, conveying the message, without saying a word, that cars were for "softies."

Upon one occasion, however, Jewell Peeke (manager of the Insurance Department of the General Conference) saw that F. D. N. appeared to be in an unusual hurry. His walking pace had been accelerated to a near run. It was considerably past the lunch hour, so Mr. Peeke gathered up his courage and stopped his car. With a sigh of gratitude, F. D. N. climbed in quickly.

"I'm glad you stopped, Brother. I'm late for a committee meeting, and——" His voice trailed away as he began examining the car, which was, in Mr. Peeke's words, "far from new." F. D. N. looked it over inside, then craning his head out the window, he examined the outside. After completing his inspection, he turned to Mr. Peeke and demanded, "Why in the world are you driving this old car?"

Mr. Peeke, somewhat taken aback, answered that he had a daughter in college, and a son in academy, and didn't feel at this point that he ought to go into debt for a new car. "I'll probably be driving old cars for a long time to come," he concluded rather sadly.

F. D. N. beamed upon him approvingly. "That's the only way to look at it—pay cash or do without. I've bought seventeen new cars during my lifetime and have paid cash for every one of them," he finished, with a flourish.

158

THE COLORFUL, WARMHEARTED INDIVIDUALIST

Taxes presented for F. D. N. the same kind of problem that they do for the rest of us who are made of more common clay. He read extensively on the subject, queried all and sundry who he thought might have helpful information, and upon at least one occasion went down for an appointment with a specialist at the Internal Revenue Bureau. Alas, the pedestrian mind of the tax man was unable to grasp the type of individual with whom he was dealing. Upon noticing that F. D. N. was listed as a minister, writer, pastor, and editor, the tax man, in his most official tone, inquired fretfully, "Now just what are you, specifically?"

"Young man, I'm a minister!" (This, with a great deal of force.)

"No, you're not. You're just a writer!" the tax man announced triumphantly.

The word "just" inserted before "writer" was too much. Drawing himself to his full height, F. D. N. announced in ringing tones, "Brother, I can marry you or bury you. Now tell me, am I a minister?"

And that settled that.

F. D. N., like all other human beings, at times adopted attitudes which, upon sober reflection, he later changed. This occurred at one point before his 1959 overseas trip. When the trip was being voted by the General Conference Committee, Jewell Peeke rose to his feet to ask who would be responsible for F. D. N. while he was overseas—the General Conference or the Review.

Surprised and somewhat annoyed, F. D. N. replied, "What difference can that possibly make?"

Mr. Peeke then explained that the difference came in the type of insurance coverage. General Conference workers are covered in foreign countries with an accident and personal disability insurance, but at that time the Review did not have this sort of coverage.

At the reporters' table during the 1946 General Conference, F. D. N. and Charles E. Weniger are conversing. Carlyle B. Haynes's familiar face is in the group.

One of the lesser known responsibilities of F. D. N. was his membership on several General Conference committees. He is seen here in session at one of the meetings of the budget committee. Elder C. L. Torrey, General Conference treasurer, is chairman of the meeting.

THE COLORFUL, WARMHEARTED INDIVIDUALIST

Apparently F. D. N. wasn't too impressed. "Well-l-l-l-l, Brother," he drawled, "I've made provision for my wife, and as far as I know the Review isn't bankrupt, so I suppose they could transport my broken body home if it should come to that!"

Mr. Peeke said no more. He considered the matter closed. What was his surprise, then, several days later, to receive a telephone call from M. E. Dawson, treasurer of the Review.

"What's this about foreign coverage when our workers go overseas? Elder Nichol has been telling me that we ought to institute this plan at the Review," he said earnestly, being totally unaware of the fact that F. D. N. had squelched Mr. Peeke on the subject a few days before.

F. D. N.'s second thoughts paid off—the Review took out the coverage—and on the trip—on July 14, 1959, at 1:30 P.M., to be exact—F. D. N. was "fortunate" enough to be involved in an automobile accident. He became the first of the Review workers to benefit from this type of coverage.

This accident, which took place on the outskirts of Wheatley, England, on the road from Oxford, hurt F. D. N.'s ankle so badly that it caused him pain for years afterward. Certainly it made the remaining part of his journey highly difficult, since he had to maneuver on and off planes, and up and down stairs on crutches. Almost any other man would have returned home. Not F. D. N. He was made of sterner stuff.

The accident, though, was not without its humorous aspects. Just before the trip one of the workers from the General Conference had visited F. D. N.'s office for the purpose of urging him to publish some material on safe driving, particularly safe driving among ministers. He chose an unfortunate time for his visit. F. D. N. was pressed almost to the breaking point with last-minute arrangements, with correspondence, with the thousand and one details that must be taken care of before the chief editor goes on an extended trip.

11

After listening briefly to the safety advocate's plea, F. D. N. pressed his hands to his temples in a typically Nicholesque gesture and burst out, "Oh, Brother, please don't harass me with safe driving just now. I have to leave this afternoon on a round-the-world trip——." The visitor got the message, and made a hasty exit.

But he didn't forget! When F. D. N. was safely home, and walking with a cane, the General Conference worker appeared once more at the editor's office. He smoothly broached the subject of an article on safe driving, purposely avoiding any reference to the previous conversation on the subject. F. D. N.'s response, as he rubbed his aching ankle, was immediate and enthusiastic.

"That's a superb idea!" he exclaimed. "Get me a good article and statistics and everything that bears on the subject."

And that's how an article on safe driving among ministers happened to appear in the *Review*.

Although resigned to the inevitable frustrations of twentieth-century living, F. D. N. never missed an opportunity to verbalize his protests to those he considered responsible for red tape and bottlenecks. The inter-mail service between the General Conference and Review and Herald buildings caused him particular bafflement. Having apparently endured as much "persecution" from this service as he deemed appropriate, he "zeroed in" during a General Conference Committee meeting.

"Brethren," he announced, rolling his r's richly, "we're living in a wonderful world of progress. It's positively amazing. I can get on a plane and get out to California in four or five hours, a distance of 3,000 miles."

Having whetted the curiosity of the committee, who realized to a man that what they had heard thus far was merely F. D. N.'s way of springing a trap, he continued, "Isn't it surprising, then, that it takes three days to get a letter through the inter-mail service from my building to your building, when they're separated by only a sidewalk?"

Whether the improvement in the inter-mail service can be attributed to his speech is problematical. But it did improve! F. D. N. was a good sport. He didn't take offense at well-deserved, skillful verbal victories, and he hugely enjoyed witnessing a nimble encounter in all good nature between two or more of his "brethren." During an Autumn Council he found himself sitting by one of the officers of the General Conference, almost at the front of the Takoma Park church. The two of them found a most important matter that they felt needed to be discussed in low tones.

This whispered conversation proved distinctly annoying to a department head who was giving his report. The department head stopped, glanced at the offenders, went on, stopped, glanced—until finally even their consciences informed them that silence was indicated. Already feeling aggrieved, the department head became unusually annoyed when the General Conference officer made a whispered comment on his report, loud enough so that all in the room could hear it. Pressed beyond endurance, the department head retorted, "Elder ———, as the surgeon said to the man on the operating table, 'that will be enough out of you!' "

F. D. N. was highly amused. *"Touché!"* he exclaimed.

In spite of his sometimes brisk, impersonal attitudes, especially in later life, just beneath the surface was an exceedingly tender heart, particularly where children were concerned. F. D. N. felt that every child was a small miracle; that every pair of small feet needed all the guidance they could be given; that every pair of small hands needed direction; that every small mind needed training. And he loved to play the role of mentor to all children, everywhere.

Only a few weeks before his death, as he was walking back to the office after lunch one day, he found that the crossing guard on Carroll Avenue, where many of the students from the John Nevins Andrews elementary church school crossed the busy intersection, had been unaccountably delayed. Without a moment's hesitation, he undertook the job of directing traffic and transporting the small students across the busy street. A General Conference friend who watched this performance in amazement telephoned him later in the day.

"I see you've added the job of policeman to your skills," he teased.

F. D. N. was a bit abashed.

"I suppose it sounds foolish and sentimental, but I get great pleasure from helping little children." After a pause, he threatened, "But don't you tell anyone about the crossing-guard incident!"

F. D. N. was more than tenderhearted; he was deeply interested in helping people. Perhaps nowhere was this more evident than in his practice of visiting the sick. Almost every Friday night and Sabbath afternoon, when he was in town, he would "make the rounds" at the Washington Sanitarium and other medical institutions, encouraging the sick and praying for them. He knew that no matter how secure and successful a person might feel when he is well, when sickness strikes, he needs added grace, strength, and faith. Throughout the years literally hundreds of patients were blessed by F. D. N.'s visits.

"There was just something about him," commented Mrs. Josephine Thurber recently. "Once when I was about to enter the sanitarium for major surgery, I was fearful and apprehensive, and almost felt that I couldn't face the ordeal. Elder Nichol came to our home when my spirits were at their lowest, shortly before I was to leave for the sanitarium. After a short visit, he prayed for me. As I listened, peace filled my heart. Every vestige of fear left me. I felt I was safe in the Lord's hands, and had no further apprehension."

THE COLORFUL, WARMHEARTED INDIVIDUALIST

When Elder Lawrence Maxwell, editor of *Guide,* had open-heart surgery in the early part of 1962, F. D. N. visited him at least five times at the National Institutes of Health in Bethesda, Maryland. On one of the visits a severe snowstorm made the route hazardous. But undeterred by radio warnings that motorists should stay off the roads if at all possible, F. D. N. made his way to NIH and Elder Maxwell's bedside.

"His visits meant a great deal to me," said Elder Maxwell in an interview. "He didn't stay long. He didn't say much. But his prayers—they were so confident, so full of living faith."

Recalling those pain-filled days, when the final outcome was less than certain medically, Elder Maxwell commented: "I felt sure that his prayers would be answered."

And they were. For him and for many, many others.

F. D. N. was colorful. F. D. N. was an individualist. F. D. N. was an intellectual. Most important, he was warmhearted. This was a key factor in making his ministry effectual.

"He who would write heroic poems should make his whole life a heroic poem."

—CARLYLE

CHAPTER 12

Personal Correspondent Par Excellence

FEW KNEW it, but F. D. N. had an enormous gift for brilliant, humorous writing. My wife and I encountered this talent for the first time during the summer of 1963 when we were traveling in Europe and the Middle East. We were on the trip to visit as many of our overseas institutions as possible, particularly in the publishing field. I wrote a weekly report for *Review* readers. On the trip F. D. N. communicated with us from time to time, writing letters that both amazed and dazzled us. We enjoyed his letters almost as much as the beauty and history of the lands we were visiting. His first letter, received in London, convulsed us with this opening paragraph, tinged with sarcasm:

"DEAR KENNETH,

"With bated breath and trembling hands, we all pounced upon your manuscript when it arrived this morning. We knew it would be a masterpiece, and we could scarcely wait for the thrill it would bring. I see you are already getting into the mood of a real traveler. We liked your little human interest side lights, including your reference to Miriam."

At this moment, with the letter before me, I can still recall with exactitude the little English hotel in one of the London suburbs, the "cage" elevator in which we had just ridden down to the tiny lobby, the extremely correct manner of the

Editorial Correspondence

8 Miles Up
Over the Atlantic
June 12, 1959

The familiar handscript of F. D. N. as it came through the mails from "eight miles up over the Atlantic."

desk clerk as he handed us the large air-mail envelope, the hasty tearing open of the letter—and then, our delighted chuckles.

If I had entertained any illusions as to the superior quality of my first "travelog," I would have been deflated in short order by F. D. N.'s tongue-in-cheek "debunking." And perhaps that was the purpose of the sage editor in chief, since travelers are all too prone to wax almost hysterically lyrical over their first encounters with new countries.

Going on, F. D. N. developed his theme.

"Cottrell is already working on the manuscript, having reserved certain space as sacred to the outpourings of our peripatetic, high-flying oracle. If you follow your present schedule of sending material, I think we are going to be able to keep up the schedule well at our end. Your manuscript arrived here about 9:30 this morning. Maybe you ought to try getting off your story Wednesday instead of Thursday. Then there will be a fair chance of its reaching here Friday morning, but I will let you be the judge of that. We will adjust whatever is necessary to be able to include each week the vivid and vivifying observations you will be offering."

Sensing that the exhilarated travelers might still be suffering a few sharp nostalgic pangs for home and the familiar routine, he included a few observations about the *Review* staff, their comings and goings.

"I will be leaving for New England in a couple of hours. So must get out of here promptly or I won't get my toothbrush packed and my shirt changed before Cottrell calls to take me to the plane. Promise [Sherman] left for Hawaii early this morning. It is the great event of her life. I am so happy she could go. Idamae [Melendy] is holding the fort. She simply must not get ill or get run over by a car until Promise gets back."

Then, reverting to one of his favorite themes—that modern "youth" (this appellation was applied to us firmly, regardless of our at-that-time impending grandparenthood) has nowadays all the rights and privileges formerly reserved for hoary age—F. D. N. wrote:

"I am so glad you can have this trip. I tell you, it is a new day, a new day. Youth is coming into its own. Please give the old slave-driving editor this bit of credit that he sold the management on the idea of a trip overseas for each of you associates. I am getting a lot of satisfaction out of this thought now that my feet are tottering and my hands shaking."

The ludicrousness of this description left us speechless. F. D. N. neither tottered nor shook—ever!

Miriam's inability to overcome her desperate fear of air travel was a source of never-ending amusement to F. D. N. Spending as much time in planes as he did, he adopted a completely relaxed, fully resigned attitude toward this, to her, unnatural form of transportation. Replying to my observation that Miriam had crossed the entire Atlantic in a state of breathless fright, he appended this note to his letter:

"P.S. DEAR MIRIAM,

"To think that you could hold your breath all those hours crossing the Atlantic and still not become cyanotic is to my mind nothing short of a modern medical miracle, but I was sure you could do the impossible. By the time you get through this trip you will be just like the rest of us, breathing easily and letting your weight down."

Alas, the latter prophecy proved false, even to this day. Subsequently, in the remaining three years of his life, F. D. N. often made sly references to the joys of flight when consciences were clear, to which Miriam never seemed to find a suitable response.

We answered this epistle so enthusiastically that, thus encouraged, F. D. N. soared to even greater heights, as this letter, addressed to Florence, Italy, testifies:

PERSONAL CORRESPONDENT PAR EXCELLENCE

"DEAR KENNETH:

"Your letter postmarked July 22 arrived this morning and Promise, by some intuitive powers she apparently possesses in common with the decipherers of the ancient Babylonian hieroglyphics, succeeded in typing out your priceless diary without delay." (This was a good-natured hint that my handwriting was legible, but little more! Actually, when a manuscript is handwritten under pressure, with corrections penciled in here and there, the challenge to a copyist is considerable!)

"As I read the manuscript, I was shaken alternately with emotions of delight and confusion—delight that I had found a new word, 'litotes,' and confusion that I should have lived so long without having made contact with this beautiful bit of transliteration from the Greek that ends up meaning simply *simple*. How simple can a poor man discover himself to be! After he has spent a lifetime trying to learn the language, he discovers that he doesn't know one of its simple words. To borrow Milton's metered line: You have become the 'cynosure of neighboring eyes.' However, I don't think I'll offer you up as a piacular sacrifice. Though I think I should, seeing you tossed in that 'simple' word with such studied casualness. Don't think that I didn't notice this. All right, now we're ready to get on, after this linguistic debauch. But, young man, be careful in the future about your words, and use only simple ones."

My "studied casualness" in the use of the word "litotes" had been a real coup, I thought. Catching F. D. N. at a loss over a word meaning happened rarely, very rarely, although those of us close to him made a habit of studying the dictionary in the hope that we might enjoy this ego-building achievement occasionally. To have stung this human dictionary into such a lengthy rebuttal was indeed a heady victory. However, the victory was short-lived, for he went on to explode any small bubble of conceit that might possibly have developed, by a devious approach to proper word usage.

171

"My eye was particularly caught with one sentence in your report: 'No one interested in the Protestant Reformation needs to be reminded that Worms was the site of Luther's Diet in 1521.' In all my reading of nutritional literature, I haven't found anything that tops this. Had your protein today?! That's pretty earthy protein, if you ask me!"

And, on the remote chance that there might still be a shred of superiority complex left, this final observation completed the ruin.

"Your manuscript is ready to go down to the typesetters. I can visualize them pressing around the linotype to learn the latest of your peregrinations. We haven't had the chance yet to get the reactions from the field, but I can imagine our subscribers panting to part the pages that they may devour your story."

F. D. N.'s wide acquaintance with literature and classical music was evident in allusions which he made to these cultural interests. Noting our plan to visit Venice, he wrote:

"We won't send you anything to Venice. By the way, I have never visited either Venice or Genoa. I have left that for the more sophisticated, exotic, and romantic tourists to take in. If you come under any one of these three subdivisions I recommend your again revising your itinerary so that you may hear your mustachioed gondolier sing the 'Miserarie' from *Il Trovatore:*

"'Ah, I have sighed to rest me, deep in the silent grave,
Ah, think of me, Ah, think of me then, my Leonora, fare-thee-well.
Out of the love I bear thee, yield I my life for thee'
(glub, glub—moans, groans—tears, splash, splash)."

The last line, obviously his own concept of the "romantic" scene, gave us conversational fodder for many miles across Italy. Did he assume that the gondolier would actually fall into the canal and swim beside his gondola for a few hundred yards?

172

PERSONAL CORRESPONDENT PAR EXCELLENCE

We'll never know; we forgot to discuss the subject with him upon our return.

When Mrs. Sherman got back from her Hawaiian trip, F. D. N. couldn't resist interpolating a comment in one of his letters to the effect that "Promise is back, large as life, looking at least ten years younger." Promise, embarrassed by this rather frank appraisal of the benefits of her vacation, inserted her *own* interpolation: "(He says that I have to write this! P. J. S.)"

In one of the last letters we received, F. D. N. allowed himself the rare luxury of sounding almost sentimental, a trait he kept in stern rein.

"We have certainly missed you over here. I wouldn't say that you left an aching void, but on the other hand, Cottrell and I have had to do a little bit of sweating and struggling to get things out on time. So we are really hoping you'll get back here safely. I think you will be wiser, and I'm sure you won't be sadder."

Then he went on with what to us was some of his most sparkling prose. He had stories for every occasion, loved to bring them out and dust them off when appropriate. At this point he set himself to the task of tying our whole trip up neatly in words, as he saw it.

"I can just picture Miriam bubbling with glee and reminiscences in the days ahead. Tell her, however, to be sure not to make the mistake of the traveler who, unfamiliar with either peasants or the Marseillaise, returned to say that of all the things she saw or heard in Europe, nothing touched her soul so much as listening to the pheasants in France singing the mayonnaise. Then, of course, there is the story of the newly rich woman telling of the beauties of Switzerland and of how she loved those two lakes, Lake Leman and Lake Geneva. When a better-informed hearer reminded her that Lake Leman and Lake Geneva are synonymous, she replied with much hauteur that she knew that, but that Lake Geneva was more synonymous than Lake Leman."

One of the first things we did after we recovered from the nearly ten weeks of travel from country to country, was to discuss the letters with their author. I remember saying to him that I hadn't dreamed he could write in this vein and I suggested that he was every bit as talented in this field as Art Buchwald or the late George Dixon. He listened with a faint smile playing about his lips. Then he replied, very seriously.

"I've always been careful to suppress this side of my nature," he said, "because I felt that I was called to do very serious work, and levity might distract from the work of the Holy Spirit. Occasionally my Irish nature creeps in in spite of me though."

Tapping his pencil on his desk, he leaned back and smiled broadly.

"It was fun to let myself go and give rein to this sort of thing. Apparently I had a good audience for it!"

At least he had an appreciative one. To have discarded the letters would have been unthinkable.

Truly F. D. N. was a personal correspondent par excellence.

CHAPTER 13

Great Defense for a Great Conviction

"NEAR THE close of the last century a young couple, living in a sparsely settled part of Australia, found by the roadside a copy of the *Review and Herald,* weekly organ of the Seventh-day Adventists. They had never heard either of the paper or of the religious body. But reading matter was at a premium, and their interest in things spiritual was great. And so they read it. One article quickened their hearts in a singular way, and they exclaimed upon finishing it: 'The person who wrote this article seems to be inspired.' The writer was Mrs. E. G. White. That conviction regarding her grew as they learned of her life and work and joined the Seventh-day Adventist Church. In turn, they instilled in the heart of their son the same conviction concerning her, a conviction he has now fully reinforced by his own study of her life and writings."

This paragraph, quoted from the dedication in F. D. N.'s book, *Ellen G. White and Her Critics,* offers at least a partial answer to the question which has at times been asked, namely: How did Francis David Nichol attain his firm faith in Ellen G. White? His clear statement as to the part played by his parents illustrates well the validity of the Biblical injunction, "Train up a child in the way he should go . . ."

To think of F. D. N.'s life and work without almost immediately putting the words "Ellen G. White" in direct juxtaposition is well-nigh impossible for most informed, adult Sev-

175

enth-day Adventists. His confidence in Ellen G. White as a possessor of the gift of prophecy was evident in all of his writing and speaking. No one did more to defend her from her critics. And since Mrs. White's writings fill such a key role in Seventh-day Adventism, it is probable that F. D. N.'s undeviating loyalty to her has had as great an influence on the denomination as anything which he did.

Besides his parents, probably another strong factor in developing F. D. N.'s faith in Mrs. White's prophetic gift was Elder J. A. Burden, the family friend and "guiding light" who was instrumental in bringing the Nichols to Loma Linda. Those who were acquainted with Elder Burden state that he had a deep, fundamental, rock-bed belief in Mrs. White's work. He was also a "man of the hour" kind of person, who, when projects were suggested, saw no giants in the way of accomplishment.

Like every growing child, young Francis undoubtedly listened to conversations between his parents and Elder Burden on long Friday evenings, on Sabbath afternoons, at worship hours. Thus the foundation of faith was laid brick by brick, stone by stone.

When as a child F. D. N. occasionally pushed Mrs. White about in her wheel chair at Loma Linda, this contact undoubtedly made an indelible impression on his deeply sensitive and strongly religious nature.

Later, at Pacific Union College, when he was enrolled in the ministerial course, his maturing intellect seems to have created in him an awareness of the importance of the prophetic gift. At least, Elder Arthur White remembers that upon one occasion young F. D. N. asked to have an afternoon's interview with Elder W. C. White (Arthur's father). What they discussed, what the purpose of the interview was, no one knows. But the long trip "down the hill" from PUC to St. Helena where Elder White lived must have had a clearly de-

176

fined purpose, for young F. D. N. seldom (if ever) wasted what he considered to be valuable time in a life already charted to accomplish more than the possible.

In later years he often sadly lamented to Elder Arthur White his immature failure to have spent a great deal of time with Elder W. C. White, Mrs. White's son. "Just think what I could have gotten from him!" F. D. N. often exclaimed. "Just think what an opportunity I missed!"

F. D. N.'s interest and faith in the Spirit of Prophecy, always vital and firm, reached full flower during research for his book *Ellen G. White and Her Critics,* published in 1951. Originally, when he was asked to prepare answers for criticisms leveled at the Spirit of Prophecy writings, it had been supposed that the answers would be contained in a series of pamphlets. But as he continued his research, and as the mountain of material grew, it was felt that the appropriate format would be a book. His purpose in this large work (703 pages) was to answer in as much detail as possible the major charges that had been brought against Mrs. White by critics.

The task he set for himself was formidable, almost frightening. The amount of research, the accurate detail, and the carefully reasoned arguments that go into a literary work of this kind are not to be undertaken lightly. Painstakingly each charge must be examined, evaluated, answered. F. D. N. had clearly defined objectives for this book, which he set forth in his usual, crisp, forthright way, in the introduction:

"I have sought to clear the air . . . so that the reader may see that Mrs. White rightly belongs on the mountain of God in the company of those who have heard and then made audible the counsels of God to men."—*Ellen G. White and Her Critics,* p. 19.

After the book was completed, F. D. N. made a statement to the special committee set up by the church to examine the manuscript. This statement is highly revelatory both of his

12

feelings and his character. Standing in his usual commanding posture, his piercing blue eyes boring into the consciences of his listeners, and gesturing to produce even greater emphasis, he declared: "I have examined all the major criticisms of Mrs. White that I could find in any book or pamphlet, checking back on all the alleged historical declarations and going to the original sources for the accurate text of all statements by Mrs. White. I have also examined many facts regarding her life. Having completed my task by preparing the extended manuscript now before you, I wish to offer this testimony: I end this work fully and irrevocably persuaded in my mind and heart that Mrs. White was what she claimed to be, a humble handmaiden of God, to whom He gave revelations, authoritative and unique, to guide and direct the Advent people in these last days."—*Why I Believe in Mrs. E. G. White*, pp. 127, 128.

This was a dramatic moment in the committee session.

In 1964, he published a smaller volume, *Why I Believe in Mrs. E. G. White*, in which he told in greater detail the story of his own family's conversion, which originally appeared in *Ellen G. White and Her Critics.*

"Nearly seventy years ago, in a village in Australia lived a young couple. They had never heard of Mrs. White, or of Seventh-day Adventists, or of the *Review and Herald*, the official organ of this Adventist Church. One day they found by the roadside a mud-spattered copy of a paper. Reading matter was scarce, so they took the paper home and dried it out by the kitchen stove. It was a copy of the *Review and Herald*. In the quiet of their little cottage amid the eucalyptus trees, they turned the pages of this unknown journal from America. They read an article on tithing. They were impressed that whoever the publishers were, they must be most earnest, sacrificial people, because they believed in giving God one tenth of their income—a tithe—besides freewill offerings. Who could these people be! They further leafed the pages, read an article by a Mrs. E. G. White, and exclaimed: 'Who is this Mrs. White? She writes as though she is inspired.'

"A few days later a villager who sold fresh vegetables stopped at their door. 'Do you know about a paper called the *Review and Herald?*' they asked. When he answered, 'Yes,' they promptly inquired: 'Do you know about a Mrs. E. G. White?' He did. 'And who is she?' they asked. He hesitated, evidently fearing if he answered them directly he might prejudice them against Adventism. But his hesitancy only made them the more insistent. Finally, fixing his eyes on them, he answered with fervor: 'She's a prophet.'

"Their interest only increased, for his words simply reinforced the conviction that had gripped them in the quiet of their humble cottage. Not long afterward they were baptized into the Seventh-day Adventist Church. Their faith in the church, and particularly in Mrs. White, only increased with the years. And that faith they passed on to their son, present editor of the *Review and Herald* and the writer of these lines."—*Why I Believe in Mrs. E. G. White,* pp. 124, 125.

Having published two books whose focal point was Ellen G. White, F. D. N. was contemplating, at the time of his death, a third book—actually two books. At the 1950 General Conference session, study had been given to the project of an exhaustive, definitive biography of Ellen G. White. The man chosen to author this monumental project was F. D. N. He accepted the challenge, declaring, "All right. But you realize that I'll need all her diaries—everything and anything that relates to her daily life, to her work. I'll have to have it all."

Under Elder Arthur White's direction, the White Estate office set about to copy all handwritten records on the typewriter. They prepared a day-by-day index, a year-by-year account of Mrs. White's comings and goings, her activities. All this, in preparation for F. D. N.'s writing assignment.

In the normal course of events the biography would have been published several years ago. That it has not yet appeared is due to the fact that the work carried on by the Seventh-day Adventist Church is complex and complicated, and has many facets. Almost at the same time that the White biography was proposed, plans were set on foot for the *Seventh-day Adventist Bible Commentary*—to be edited by F. D. N. This staggering project, already described, absorbed his every moment until 1958.

The biography of Ellen G. White will be written—but not by F. D. N.

His books and sermons on the subject of Mrs. White form what we perhaps might term the "public" side of his commitment to the Spirit of Prophecy. Another side, less well-known though not "private" in any sense, was his position as a life member, a life trustee, of the Ellen G. White Estate. The Estate, formed in 1915 after the death of Mrs. White, is described in the Seventh-day Adventist *Yearbook* as follows:

"An organization formed in harmony with the trust created in the will of the late Ellen G. White, to act as her agent in the custody of her writings, and in the promotion of their continued publication in all lands."

There are nine trustees, some elected for life, others elected for four-year terms. Whenever a member dies, or for some reason is unable to serve, the remaining members elect his successor. Elder Arthur L. White, grandson of Mrs. E. G. White, is secretary of the Estate, which is housed on the ground floor of the General Conference building. The trustees take their responsibilities seriously, well aware of the far-reaching consequences of their decisions and actions.

It is safe to assert, I believe, that no one felt this sacred responsibility more keenly than F. D. N. He served a kind of apprenticeship during the 1940's, when a "Defense Literature Committee" was formed, and then a subcommittee, of which

180

The trustees of the Ellen G. White Estate in 1963. Left to right, seated: W. P. Bradley, F. D. N., A. L. White, D. A. Delafield. Standing: G. A. Huse, F. A. Mote, W. G. C. Murdoch, R. S. Watts, Neal C. Wilson.

F. D. N. was a member. The primary task of this group was to formulate answers to questions regarding the Spirit of Prophecy writings. It is easy to see how the work done during this time led naturally to the publication of the books we have already discussed.

In April of 1950 F. D. N.'s name appears for the first time in the minutes of the White Estate as an alternate member. In 1952 he was made a life member.

During these years the late Elder A. V. Olson was the president, or chairman, of the Estate, terms which are used interchangeably. When Elder Olson died in April of 1963, F. D. N. was elected president. This manifestation of confidence by the other trustees touched him deeply. It was axiomatic with him that any item dealing with the White Estate had high priority on his time.

Elder Arthur White summed up F. D. N.'s place with the group, when he said with obviously deep feeling, "We never had a better friend."

181

*"Thou wert my guide,
philosopher, and friend."*

—ALEXANDER POPE
"Essay on Man"

CHAPTER 14

The World of F.D.N.'s
Friendships

EVERY Seventh-day Adventist was his friend—that's the way F. D. N. looked at it. When he sat down to write his editorials he visualized himself as composing a letter to a large but intimate circle of friends, a circle who wanted to hear from him, even though they might not always be completely happy with the contents of his "letters"! At camp meetings when he was not speaking or preparing to speak, he strolled about the grounds visiting with the "saints," as he often referred to them privately. And he was so well-known, with his silvery white hair and his crisp, incisive speech, that he seldom had to say, "I'm Brother Nichol."

Although he considered everyone his friend, a few people became rather special to him because of circumstances, shared experiences, or other reasons.

There was a young couple in Tennessee with whom he often stayed when he was in that part of the country. He enjoyed their home—set in a rural, wooded area. They, in turn, enjoyed their association with him. And so they conceived the idea that they would, when finances permitted, build a "motel cabin" on their spacious, tree-shaded property, and assign it permanently to Elder and Mrs. Nichol, in the hope that someday, for weeks at a time, it would be occupied by these cherished friends. If F. D. N. had known of their plan—which he didn't, for he died before they had a chance to tell him about it—he doubtless would have urged them to spend the money on something else—to help build a new church or to finance a student through school. But he would have been vastly pleased that the scheme had occurred to them.

There also were the Burnhams, of Maitland, Florida, who kept the latchstring permanently out for him when responsibilities called him to that part of the Southland.

And there were the Stanley Steiners, a young minister and his wife, who regarded him as their *very* special friend.

And there was Eugene Durand, one of his Hyattsville "boys," who not only became a minister but a missionary.

And Thomas Green, also of Hyattsville, whose ministerial success gratified F. D. N.

And there was . . . But the list is endless. One need only mention his name in any group of Seventh-day Adventists and someone will say, "Why, he always stayed at our house, and he took a special interest in each one of the children, sending them letters at various important times of their lives." It is impossible, then, to recount all the personal friendships. As typical, I have selected, somewhat arbitrarily, three or four.

T. K. Martin possessed perhaps the perfect personality to act as a foil for that of F. D. N. They met as young men together at the Review. Their children were contemporaries (all girls!). They shared the same firm faith in the Seventh-day Adventist Church and the importance of the work of the Lord. And they shared rare moments of relaxation together—rare because F. D. N. was a man to whom work was relaxation and effort was fun. Children, though, must be given consideration, so on Sabbath afternoons in the long-ago days, F. D. N. would often put Viriginia into her little wagon, pull her down the street to the Martin home, and shout loudly, "Is anybody home?"

When somebody *was* home—which was nearly always—

T. K. would put his two little girls into their own wagon, and away the small caravan would go—to the woods at the foot of the street, where the little girls played happily while F. D. N. and T. K. had long, fascinating conversations about "The Truth."

The children have grown up; the woods have disappeared; houses have been built; but the memories are still there.

"How he increased my vocabulary!" T. K. says with a grin. "He'd use all those big words which, to him, were natural and commonplace. I'd listen, and try not to seem overawed or mystified, then at the first possible moment I'd look them up in the dictionary."

Once in a while apparently it would occur to F. D. N. that other people had all sorts of hobbies and recreational activities. Dimly sensing that not everyone enjoyed an eighteen-hour workday, he would at times attempt to discover just what it was that was so fascinating in the way "the other half" lived. A case in point was his one and only attempt at fishing in the East. During one of the summer vacation weeks at the shore he suggested to T. K. that the two of them arise early the next morning and go fishing. Amazed, since he knew F. D. N. was a vegetarian, T. K. agreed.

Full of bustle and plans, F. D. N. made arrangements to rent a small rowboat. "Now here's how it works, T. K.," he said. "The man who rents the boat will tow us out attached to his motorboat. Then we'll put down an anchor and stay there as long as we wish. If for some reason we want to come in, all we have to do is prop up one of our oars in a certain way and he'll cruise around and tow us back in!"

Apparently sensing T. K.'s less than wild enthusiasm, F. D. N. burst into laughter. "Oh, oh, I forgot—you're a very bad sailor, Terence! Well, you'll just have to plan to exert mind over matter!"

Weakly, T. K. agreed, pleading only that he be allowed to

take along his sketchbook. Magnanimously, F. D. N. thought that this might be appropriate, inferring that T. K.'s artistic soul might need some nourishment that the rather plebeian business of catching fish would fail to provide.

Armed with a small can of worms, they tiptoed out of the cabin the next morning, leaving the womenfolk and the girls sound asleep. Since their less than elegant rowboat contained some water, they took off their shoes and rolled up their trousers—and away they went.

Anchored some distance from shore, they soon discovered that the waves which at a distance had looked so small and harmless were actually large and dangerous. Up and down went the boat. Sideways went the boat. Up and down *and* sideways went the boat. Not one whit daunted, F. D. N. announced that he had "a strike"—and pulled from the watery depths a most amazing creature—one which kept flopping about on the bottom of the boat and emitting hoarse, croaking sounds.

F. D. N., no ichthyologist, was baffled. "What in the world is *this?*" he inquired, keeping his bare feet well out of reach of the squirming, slimy sea creature.

"I would think," T. K. announced with dignity, in spite of his rather ashen face, "that it simply has to be a croaker."

Digesting this information for a moment, F. D. N. announced triumphantly, "Well, think what a sore throat he must have, with that kind of noise." And he promptly threw the complaining fish back into the water.

They settled themselves to wait, T. K. at one end of the boat, facing forward, and F. D. N. at the other end, facing backward. Up and down and sideways they went, jostled by the gentle waves.

Hearing what he considered to be a suspicious noise, F. D. N. turned around and inquired sharply, "Terence, what are you doing?"

"Nothing at all," insisted T. K.

186

THE WORLD OF F. D. N.'S FRIENDSHIPS

"I know I heard you gagging. And you'll make *me* sick if you don't look out."

More silence.

Then, meekly, F. D. N. inquired, "Shall we signal for our pilot or shall we try to row back?"

Groaning with nausea, T. K. gasped, "Put up the oar. Let's be towed in!"

And thus ended the half-hour fishing expedition. Two green faces. One croaker.

In later years the shared outings became fewer, but the friendship remained firm.

One day during the Civil War Centennial celebrations, F. D. N. strolled into T. K.'s office and said: "I see by the paper that they're going to re-enact the battle of Antietam, near Sharpsburg, Maryland. Let's go up and take it in!" (History had been one of F. D. N.'s abiding interests ever since his senior year at Pacific Union College when he'd filled in for an ailing history teacher.)

The idea sounded good to T. K. "Let's!" was his enthusiastic response.

Arriving on the scene, they discovered that thousands of people were milling about the old battlefield; also that only persons in blue or gray uniforms could be "where the action was." Although T. K.'s photographer's press pass entitled him to be right in the thick of things, he needed a uniform to authenticate his activities. And all the costumes in town had long before been rented out for the occasion. Not to be defeated, however, the two adventurers managed to find a Confederate cap for T. K. Off he went into "battle," cameras over his shoulder, while F. D. N. waved enthusiastically from the spectators' grandstand.

And this was their last major outing together.

One of the best known of F. D. N.'s friendships with people younger than himself was his relationship with Elder John

Loor. F. D. N.'s editorial in the June 3, 1965, *Review and Herald* gave the details of how it all came about, and since there are many unique facets to the story, I am including the editorial here. It was in two parts, the first part of which commented on a youth congress held in Atlantic City, N.J. On Sabbath morning more than 16,000 people attended. Wrote F.D.N.:

"The Sabbath morning speaker was not one of our mature ministers, full of years and experience—and we always thank God for the years and the experience. Instead, he was one of our younger ministers; to be exact, he was only 37 years old. Why should we mention his age? Because we think it is significant in this context. Nor did he look a day older. And did God speak through the young man? He did. Calmly, undramatically, he brought to that assembled host of youth a message for them in these days, a message that appealed to them to seek for the right values and for the things that would abide. All of our hearts were moved, whether young or old.

"We first met him when he was only four years old. Each Sabbath morning he sat beside his mother in a little church not far from Takoma Park where we had the privilege, as a kind of extra activity, of serving as pastor. We knew well the home, a divided home. We have his permission to say here that his father is an alcoholic. Sometimes the father was missing for extended periods.

"The awful depression decade was upon us. In a home like his, money was not simply scarce, it was often nonexistent. We thank God for the sacrificial little church that was willing to raise money for tuition for children who could not afford otherwise to attend. Yes, we enrolled him in our church school in Takoma Park. And he stayed there right through to graduation from the eighth grade, the most impressionable years of all. Those who were wage earners in the depression decade can appreciate what we mean when we say that money seemed pitifully scarce for most people. But there was money ready

F. D. N. and John Loor in 1962 at the General Conference session in San Francisco. Elder Loor was a small boy in the Hyattsville, Maryland, church when Elder Nichol was pastor.

from dedicated church members who felt as much passionate concern for children nearby, as they did for heathen children far away.

"Came the day when this young man graduated from the ministerial course at our college here in Takoma Park and began that slow ascent up the ladder of the ministry toward efficient and effective service. Now we were listening to him preach. He preached with power, cogency, and appeal. For a moment we were there in the auditorium listening intently, and then again we seemed to be far away visiting a poor little home, broken and blighted by drink, with a mother supported by a sacrificial church so she could send her boy to the church school. It was a very great day for us.

"Nothing has ever provided more striking proof of the worth of our church schools. May God give to all of us, both ministers and laity, a greater sense of the importance of having all our children in our church schools. It can be done. It should be done. It must be done, if we are to measure up to our full responsibility for those who will come after us.

189

"We are not here writing a glowing advertisement for a particular young man. God forbid. Rather, we would eulogize our dedicated church school teachers for the impress they quietly make on the hearts of the children under their care. We well remember the times when Miriam Tymeson, long in charge of our Takoma Park school, told us of her personal interest in this young boy and how he had the possibilities of a preacher, so she thought; and she was right! The church school training set him in that direction.

"We must never despair in the face of the most discouraging and forbidding circumstances, and most surely those were the circumstances in the home in which this boy grew up. To our fellow brethren in the ministry we would say: Find hope and possibilities even where there seem to be none. God still lives and His angels still guard little children and encourage faithful mothers."

That's how F. D. N. saw John Loor. But what about the latter? How did he, as a little boy, then as a young man, and now as church pastor, see F. D. N.? In a letter he set forth this picture:

"I first remember Elder Nichol when I was growing up in the Review and Herald Memorial church in Hyattsville, Maryland. It seemed to me that he always looked the same. He looked so impressive with his silver hair and he never seemed to look any older with the passage of time.

"As a youngster and then as a youth I well remember his unswerving stand for principle. I also remember his emphasis on the fact that the Seventh-day Adventist Church is indeed a movement raised up of God. While attending the Hyattsville church as a boy, I remember Elder Nichol visiting the various Sabbath school divisions. He seemed to have a special appreciation of red-haired little girls, and I recall his saying that this always reminded him of his wife, whose red hair he loved very much.

"One day Elder Nichol came to visit my mother while we were living in Brentwood, Maryland. I was in the fourth grade at the time and Elder Nichol strongly urged my mother to take me out of public school and put me into church school. For this, I am deeply grateful. I believe that God used him to be a blessing to me.

"This was also in the depression days and I remember that in the fall of the year when Elder Nichol used to come around, people always knew he was going to be asking for money— especially for the church school.

"Coming further down the way, I remember the occasion of the twenty-fifth anniversary of the Hyattsville, Maryland, church (Dec. 28 and 29, 1956). Interestingly enough, I had come back to pastor that church in which I grew up as a boy. On that occasion it was a real thrill to stand by the side of Elder Nichol with the challenge to carry on the work he had started there when I was a boy.

"Later in 1956, Elder Nichol had part in my ordination at the Potomac Conference camp meeting in New Market, Va.

"Through the years, he has stopped in to see us in our various locations. He came to see us in Dallas, Texas, and also here in Arlington, California. We enjoyed calling him 'Uncle Francis.'

"Four years ago (1962) at General Conference in San Francisco, we again stood on the platform together as he interviewed me after a presentation on the screen of my life and the importance of church school.

"In April of 1965, we had one of the nicest occasions together at the Atlantic City Youth's Congress. It was my privilege to preach the Sabbath morning service on that occasion. Following it, Elder Nichol came up and put his arms around me and wept tears of joy. It meant a great deal to him and his appreciation of my sermon meant a great deal to me.

"When he came to stay with us he always traveled light.

He carried only one small suitcase and wore the same suit for his speaking appointments, yet always looked distinguished.

"We always enjoyed his sense of humor. One time he told of his experience as a young man when he was derisively called a 'cabbage eater.' He said he would rather be a cabbage eater than a cow's graveyard.

"Elder Nichol truly was a great person and we feel ever grateful to have been able to share in his personality, guidance, and dedication. We shall forever cherish these memories."

Eli and Samuel; F. D. N. and John Loor.

F. D. N. proved that he could be a good "layman" as well as an outstanding pastor. As one of the elders of the large Sligo church, he threw himself into all its projects with typical zeal, particularly if the project had to do with raising or giving money. Each pastor, during his term of leadership, often gave thanks for F. D. N.'s loyalty. The last of these men was William Loveless, F. D. N.'s pastor at the time of his death.

Since Elder Loveless was in his early thirties when he became pastor, F. D. N. found a ready-made "victim" for his dire predictions that youth could not safely be trusted with responsible office or momentous decisions. Tongue in cheek, he'd remind his pastor, of whom he became very fond, that he must strive to avoid at all times the pitfalls of his extreme (to F. D. N.!) youth.

Elder Loveless, a good sport, and willing to enter into the spirit of the "dialog," returned F. D. N.'s affection, and counted on him for solid backing. When the church launched a large fund-raising campaign to build a church school, every member was asked to make a sacrificial pledge, to continue for at least three years. Some pledged; others did not. Incredibly, F. D. N. was the largest contributor, in actual cash.

"He gave an initial sum, which was considerable," Elder Loveless reminisced in an interview. "Then when the pledges got behind, he gave more and then more, until the total was—

well, he wouldn't want me to say. He actually asked me to promise that I would never publicly state the amount."

As far as other church projects went, the pastor knew that he could always call on F. D. N. for a little extra gift if things "bogged down."

"He'd pay his pledge for the organ, or air conditioning, or whatever—then he would telephone me later and say, 'Now, my brother, I'm all up to date with my pledge, but if you need just a wee bit more to put you over the top, don't hesitate to call on me.' "

Elder Loveless *didn't* hesitate!

The two men exchanged brief letters every now and then, typical of which are these:

"November 17, 1964

"DEAR ELDER NICHOL:

"Many thanks for your generosity in sending me *Church Budget Development*. When you give your pastor something, even though it may seem insignificant to you, the least he can do is tell you he appreciates it. By the way, two additional volumes to the set of commentaries have come out since you so graciously donated a set to the pastor's study.

"Sincerely,

"WILLIAM LOVELESS"

F. D. N. could take a hint. On November 25 he answered:

"DEAR BROTHER LOVELESS:

"In response to your very subtle hint and suggestion, here are the two books: *Bible Dictionary* and *Source Book* for the Sligo church.

"Sincerely,

"F. D. NICHOL"

Help in the field of finance, however necessary it is, and however dear to the heart of a pastor, isn't the only kind of help that is appreciated. F. D. N. gave other kinds to his young pastor.

13

"When the church board would be pulling this way and that, and would seem to be getting off the track, Elder Nichol would listen to all the discussion, then he'd get to his feet and make a speech so analytical, so reasoned, so well thought out, that he saved the day more than once," said Elder Loveless.

"Also, I could always count on him to make little promotional speeches, on very short notice. He and I had an agreement during the last couple of years that I wouldn't ask him to serve on any committees, he was so tied up with so many projects, but he said he'd make promotional speeches when I needed them. And I needed them often!"

Elder Loveless felt, on September 17, 1964, that he ought to express his feelings in a letter. In part, he said:

"Your keen interest in the spiritual needs of Sligo church has always been deeply appreciated not only by me but by my predecessors. If you sincerely raise the question of your membership on the board of elders, I sincerely urge you to accept the invitation of the nominating committee to continue as an elder of the Sligo church. Your resounding speeches in favor of some church program are worth more than you know to me and to our church. Your counsel, judgment, and wisdom, I feel, are indispensable, and unless you get cantankerous and refuse to serve, I hope you will be on our board as long as I am around."

Not a man given to excessive praise, F. D. N. occasionally allowed himself to express appreciation for the efforts of others. He must have felt that something of the sort was called for in the letter which he wrote to his pastor on October 14, 1964, for the last paragraph reads:

"You are doing a good work and keeping things humming at the church. I am encouraged about you, even though you have the handicap of being young. But time will remedy that —oh, how soon!"

A Friday night ritual, whenever F. D. N. was in town, was

194

a telephone call to Elder Loveless. About nine o'clock, or nine-fifteen, the telephone would ring in the parsonage. One or the other of the Lovelesses would announce, without picking up the receiver—"That's Elder Nichol!"

With the formality which he felt the pastor deserved (F. D. N. never, never called him "Bill" as do so many others) F. D. N. would usually begin the conversation this way: "Well, my brother, I've been away on a little trip, and I thought I'd better call and see if I'm still in good and regular standing in my church."

And the unfailing answer from his pastor would come back: "Well, our board *is* working on your name. I haven't heard just what they've decided to do about it!"

Then, with the small talk concluded, the two men would discuss theological problems, members who needed help, or F. D. N. might share some of his experiences in his earlier life. They'd chat, perhaps for half an hour. F. D. N.'s pastor misses those chats. He said so.

For the first few years that I was associated with F. D. N. at the *Review*, my wife was so overawed by him that she seldom ventured more than a timid, restrained comment in his presence. As time went on, however, and he invited her to write The Art of Living . . . When You're Young column, she lost her timidity and expressed her opinions rather freely and forcefully. In fact, they had long, involved conversations about a wide range of topics. Deliberately she'd add a new word to her vocabulary every now and then, determined to put him to rout. When she succeeded her sense of triumph was heady.

Reader response to her Art of Living column was mostly favorable—and fairly large. F. D. N. was delighted. But he used to indulge in a good deal of head-wagging about the "dangers" of "Miriam's becoming inflated"—even though he knew that from week to week she was sure that she'd never have another worth-while idea to write about. Every now and then he'd state in his most disarming manner that he had "editorials written for the next three months." Then, knowing full well my wife's tendency toward being merely one step ahead of disaster, he'd ask, his blue eyes lighting up with deceptive innocence, "Let's see now, Miriam, where do you stand on columns?"

Through gritted teeth, she'd often have to admit that she was just then producing copy for the current issue. It was a game they both enjoyed playing.

F. D. N. pretended that birthdays were a bore and should be ignored—especially his own. But the fact that his occurred on February 14, Valentine's Day, made this difficult to enforce. Frequently friends would put on a little celebration. On one occasion of this kind Miriam composed a poem—to use the term loosely—which pleased him mightily. He insisted on having a copy of the following "immortal" attempt:

"Ode to F. D. N. on His Valentine Birthday

" 'Tis custom, I find, that down through the ages,
In story and poem and songs by the sages
Earth's memorable days are recounted and touted.
When Attila the Hun was having his fun,
When the fiddle of Nero brought Rome's future to zero,
When Romulus and Remus sans wolf were in extremis,
When brash Samson fell under Delilah's base spell,
When George crossed the Delaware with Hessians all
unaware,
When Abe read by firelight, thus straining his eyesight,
When Jack swam the waves, his comrades to save—
Apparently, always, a man with a quill
Recorded the deed, posterity to thrill.
But sad to relate, by a queer twist of fate

THE WORLD OF F. D. N.'S FRIENDSHIPS

The writers were napping at a certain great happ'ning;
A person unique, of whose gifts we now speak,
  With brain unexcelled,
  With sharp wit as well,
  With outstanding good looks,
  With the skill to write books—
His initials, F. D. N., are known to all men!
(The temptation is great to wax most rhapsodical—
But the only thing rhyming with *that* is methodical!)
  So to shorten this lyric
  Of praise panegyric
  In lieu of adulation
  And much congratulation
  We simply shall say
  A Most Happy Birthday!"

The world of F. D. N.'s friendships—what a delightful world it was! Not only was it a stimulating, inspiring world, it was a safe world, a world where confidences were never betrayed, where explanations were never necessary.* On this the friends who shared it speak unitedly, and with feeling. He was so much a part of his friends' lives; he was always there when he was needed. He always would be—wouldn't he?

---

* See Appendix L for letter of condolence to a friend whose husband had died.

"Let me go quickly like a candle light
Snuffed out just at the heyday of its glow!
Give me high noon—and let it then be night!
Thus would I go."

—JOHN G. NEIHARDT
"Let Me Live Out My Years"

CHAPTER 15

Day of Sudden Darkness

JUNE 3, 1966.

Blue skies, white clouds, cool breezes, and spring blossoms combined to make Takoma Park especially beautiful on this day. Nowhere was there a hint of the tragedy that was soon to strike. This was Friday, the preparation day for the Sabbath, always a busy time. And this was a particularly busy season, with the General Conference session less than two short weeks away.

The day before, Thursday, June 2, began with a meeting called by F. D. N. to work out the final details for producing the General Conference Bulletins. At nine-thirty, F. D. N. presided in the Review and Herald chapel over his temporary staff of about 30 people. These included his two associates, R. F. C. and K. H. W., the editorial secretaries, Promise Sherman and Idamae Melendy, with additional secretarial help to be pressed into service for "the duration"—Vada Gentry, Areta Perkins, and Esther Adels. Then there were the heads of all the departments—art, engraving, pressroom, typeroom, proofroom, copyroom—all the multiplicity of "rooms" which make up the publishing business. There were several writers who would do the "story of the day at Detroit," such as Lawrence Maxwell, Don Neufeld, Merwin Thurber, and H. M. Tippett.

F. D. N. was in rare good form. Nothing so stimulated him

HIS INITIALS WERE F. D. N.

as the Bulletin planning. He was figuratively licking his lips
in anticipation of the frantic deadlines which must be met,
the split-second timing, the meticulous planning—all of this
was the meat and drink of this man who loved challenges.

Considerable banter went on, particularly between Lawrence Maxwell, no slow man himself with repartee, and
F. D. N. His blue eyes sparkling, his white hair gleaming,
F. D. N. topped every remark with an even wittier observation of his own. Good-naturedly, he "threatened" the staff,
promising every kind of dire "punishment" if there were any
slip-ups.

After every question had been answered, the stimulating
session came to an end about eleven o'clock. Then F. D. N.,
R. F. C., and I adjourned to our editorial offices on the third
floor, to finalize on our own schedules. As we discussed together the first Bulletin, and the material to be included, I
noticed that F. D. N. was writing on his mimeographed schedule sheet several items that were already there. Rather
hesitantly (for I did not wish to embarrass him) I inquired,
"Chief, why are you doing that? Those items are already on the
sheet."

There was a moment of silence as F. D. N. confirmed my
observation. Then he burst out, "What in the world makes a
man do a trick like that?" As he erased the offending lines, he
began to rationalize his conduct, since any weakness in himself he found well-nigh unforgivable.

"After all," he philosophized, "I shouldn't be at all surprised if some of the Supreme Court Justices can't even remember where their umbrellas are—but that doesn't mean
that they don't remember every line of the cases they're studying. They're pretty sharp boys." He glanced at me rather
covertly, then went on, "I think I still can carry a line of
argument through, perhaps better than I ever could. I think I
can organize, collate, and mobilize material without any hesi-

200

tancy, and do a better job than when I was younger——" His voice trailed off as if waiting for reassurance.

Both R. F. C. and I provided this, promptly and sincerely, having just examined thoroughly a church-state address that F. D. N. was to deliver at Andrews University the following weekend. "I only wish I could do a fraction as well as you, no matter what the assignment," I declared.

Obviously cheered by the hero worship of his associates (he *knew* that both of us respected him highly), F. D. N. concluded the discussion by declaring that he had recently asked Dr. George Harding, whom he admired intensely, if a few lapses of memory meant anything serious, and had been told that they did not.

I wondered at the time why such a small incident disturbed such a great man. Was he conscious then that something was wrong? No one will ever know. We separated—F. D. N. going over to the General Conference building on a business matter, R. F. C. and I getting back to our routines.

The day wore on. Lunch was followed by a meeting of resident members of the Sabbath School Lesson Committee, of which both R. F. C. and I were members, in Committee Room B in the General Conference building.

At about two-thirty during the committee, Idamae Melendy, one of the editorial secretaries, tiptoed into the room through the door farthest from the chairman and asked me to step out into the hall. I thought at first that this was merely a routine interruption—a schedule mix-up or some other such crisis—but then I noticed Miss Melendy's face. It was pale and tense.

"What's the matter, Idamae?" I asked.

She could hardly get the words out. "Elder Nichol has had a probable heart attack, and has been admitted to the Washington Sanitarium," she whispered.

"You can't mean it!" I protested.

"I'm afraid it's true. Mrs. Nichol called Promise and said that because General Conference is coming so soon the staff should know at once." Miss Melendy looked at me as if to say, "What shall we do now?"

"How many people know about this?" I asked.

"Thus far, only you, Promise, and I, at the Review."

"All right. I'll tell Elder Cottrell, but then let's not tell anyone else. You know how Elder Nichol is. He wouldn't want people talking about his illness, and speculating as to what may happen. It may turn out to be just a scare. If it is, and he's back at his desk on Monday, he wouldn't want anyone to know he'd been sick. Better that no word go out until we know something more definite."

With that, I went back into the committee room, and tried to organize my thoughts. R. F. C. was across the table from me, so in about ten minutes I pushed a note across to him, asking that he step out into the hall. When I broke the disquieting news, he was as shocked as I had been. And he agreed instantly that silence was the best plan, for the moment.

We both went back to the Lesson Committee. R. F. C. stayed until it was over, but I left after about half an hour.

Later, back in our editorial offices at the Review, the four of us on the staff agreed to keep the bad news a secret as long as possible. R. F. C. and I would, at five-thirty, go together to the Washington Sanitarium to check on F. D. N.'s condition. We knew that he would be desperately concerned about the *Review*, because of the extra issues so soon to be produced, and we wanted to reassure him. Besides that, of course, there were endless questions running through our minds. How had it happened? What really *had* happened? All we knew was that he had been stricken while walking home to lunch.

The hour until "quitting time" at five-thirty dragged interminably. All of us on the staff tried to proceed with our responsibilities. It wasn't easy. Days later one of the copyreaders told me that she had seen me in the Review library late Thursday afternoon, doing some necessary research. She was, she said, surprised at my pale, sad expression. Thinking that possibly I was wrestling with a personal problem, and not wishing to be "nosy," she had said nothing about it at the time.

At five-thirty R. F. C. rode with me to the sanitarium. Dreading what we might find, we rather hesitantly pushed open the door of F. D. N.'s room on the third floor. The sight was not reassuring. The stricken man was in an oxygen tent. Mrs. Nichol stood by anxiously. But as we approached the high white hospital bed, both R. F. C. and I were impressed that he looked good. And he was—himself! His voice was strong, his eyes alert. I made the usual rather feeble approach to situations of this kind, "What are you doing here?" Then I added something like, "I never thought I'd see iron-man Nichol prone in a hospital bed."

Mrs. Nichol began to explain. "He had stopped at Savage's grocery store and was walking home when he felt a sudden, severe pain in his chest. He should have sat down, or lain down——" and she glanced at the recumbent figure with the loving resigned acceptance of many years—"but instead he kept on walking, slowly."

F. D. N. took up the story. "I was only four blocks from home, and why in the world would I want to make a scene?"

Mrs. Nichol was not to be deterred. "Well, you should have! But be that as it may, when he got home, and I realized the kind of pain he was in, I got a doctor—over his vigorous protests—and we brought him here in an ambulance as quickly as possible."

F. D. N. sniffed disdainfully. He seemed to consider the use of an ambulance as somehow humiliating, although later he commented to a visitor that it was quite exciting. "The sirens were screaming, and everything!"

Noting that the patient was "down but not out," I re-

203

marked, "I suppose you immediately diagnosed your own condition?"

"Young man," F. D. N. announced, "it didn't take super intelligence to recognize a heart attack." The unspoken inference was plain: "Did I edit a medical journal all those years for nothing?"

Even F. D. N.'s determined cheerfulness, though, sagged a little as the minutes went by. Both R. F. C. and I assured him over and over that all was well; that the work at the Review was so well planned that there was no need for him to worry; that we would carry on with all the energy and skill we could command.

He believed us. But dear F. D. N.—through all the years, no matter what their age, he always thought his associates were boys trying to do a man's work. They *needed* him. And he needed to be needed.

Before we left, R. F. C. offered a short prayer. We started for the door, then I turned back for a final word. "Remember that only the four of us on the staff know you're down. If this proves to be just a false alarm, and you're back at work Monday, there'll be no need for explanations of any kind."

F. D. N. gazed at me for a moment, then quietly asked, "But, Kenneth, how will you explain my demise?"

Startled, not knowing whether he was serious, or whether this was just another example of his irrepressible humor, I tried to reassure him. "Why, chief, you've always said you'd be around to write the back page notice for your associates! We're still counting on that." (The reference was to a standing bit of rather grisly banter among the editors. The death of some workers is announced on the back page, as readers of the *Review* are aware.)

F. D. N. looked amused and pleased. "That's right," he said softly. "That still stands."

Walking out to my car, R. F. C. and I tried to tell ourselves that it couldn't *possibly* be serious. We talked about "indigestion," "pleurisy," "neuritis," "mild coronaries"—all terms that sound less frightening. But still there was the nagging fear, "What if . . ."

Before leaving the office we had agreed that Mrs. Sherman would alert Andrews University to the fact that F. D. N. might not be able to give his address on church-state relationships the next weekend. We felt that while the specific nature of his illness need not be mentioned, in all fairness since the occasion at Andrews had been planned long and carefully, those who were counting on the address (as well as several other appointments) should be kept informed. The telephone call created a bit of chaos at Andrews—typical of the general chaos to come less than twenty-four hours later.

Friday morning—the blue-and-white-and-beautiful Friday morning—dawned, with the usual flurry of activity and responsibility. At our home we rushed around trying to get all the members of the family off, on time, to their various destinations. I said to my wife, Miriam, that perhaps we could see F. D. N. in the evening. But on the chance that only members of the family or associates might be admitted to the room, Miriam decided to write him a note. During the years that she had been writing the Art of Living column for the *Review* she had often sent notes to him, calling his attention to news items, expressing her opinion on this or that doctrinal point— or just chatting. She felt that "a note from Miriam" might be a "cheerer-upper."

But she was in such a rush! She *had* to be at school at eight-fifteen, before the hundreds of students came thundering into the school building. "I'll write the note when I get home, then you can take it to the hospital tonight," she said.

Momentarily satisfied with her decision, she continued with the regular morning routine. But soon she felt a compulsion to write immediately, to tell F. D. N. of our good wishes for his recovery. The clock was ticking, ticking. Time was flying! But suddenly she threw down her comb and raced for the study and a piece of note paper. Standing, then, by the dresser in the bedroom, she hurriedly dashed off a note. It was no masterpiece, just a statement of sincere affection, and a wish for his speedy recovery.

"I'd like you to leave this note at the hospital for Elder Nichol as you go to work," Miriam said.

Surprised, I retorted, "I thought you'd decided to write it this afternoon."

"Well, I changed my mind. Please leave it on your way to the office."

"All right—if it means that much to you."

When I arrived at the san, F. D. N. was sleeping, so after talking to the medical personnel on the floor, I tiptoed in and put the note on the dresser. "Be sure he sees it," I said to the nurse. Later, when Mrs. Nichol came in, she read it to him. He seemed pleased.

About ten o'clock Mrs. Sherman burst into my office, her face wreathed in smiles. "Have you heard the good news?"

I was afraid to be too optimistic. Cautiously, I asked, "No, what news?"

"Mrs. Nichol just telephoned to say that the EKG's [electrocardiograms] taken this morning look pretty good. The doctors are saying that Elder Nichol may be able to go to General Conference after all—possibly even to Andrews University next weekend!"

"That *is* good news." It was so good that it was hard for me to believe. It was far out of line with what a doctor had told me only two hours before, as I was leaving F. D. N.'s room. "Elder Nichol is a very sick man," the physician had stated. "He must have absolutely no visitors."

Do telephones have a special sound when they carry tragic news? Does the bell have a particularly melancholy sound? Or is it all in the imagination? Telephones ring constantly in editorial offices; they jangle from morning until night. There should have been nothing special about the ring of my office phone about eleven-forty-five. And yet it was different—heartbreakingly different. The voice on the other end of the line was that of C. E. Palmer, general manager of the Review.

"Has Elder Figuhr called you?"

"No, what about?"

"Elder Nichol just died."

Stunned, I asked, "Are you sure?"

"I'm afraid so. Elder Figuhr just called me. The doctor called him from the san."

"It's really true, then?" I persisted, unable and unwilling to believe news so terrible.

"I'm afraid it is."

It was. Though the sky was still blue to the general public, it seemed dark indeed to the Review family.

"*He is gone who seem'd so great.—*
Gone, but nothing can bereave him
Of the force he made his own
Being here."

—TENNYSON

"Ode on the Death of the Duke of Wellington"

CHAPTER 16

Final Services for
a Fallen Giant

FOR A MOMENT after hearing the sad news that F. D. N. was dead, I sat at my desk, almost refusing to believe, as if by denying the fact I could somehow bring him back. Then, hurrying into the hall, I attempted to find R. F. C. He was out of the building momentarily, but T. K. Martin, art director of the Review, was coming down the hall.

"Have you heard the tragic news?"

"What news?" asked T. K., dear friend of F. D. N. through many years.

"Elder Nichol just died."

"Oh, no!" he exclaimed.

H. M. Tippett, associate book editor, happened by. As I told him the news, he paled and sat down in a nearby chair, in a near faint.

And that was the reaction all through the plant, as the dreadful news spread. Little groups of people gathered here and there—in the library, the proofroom, the typeroom, the engraving department. Work came to a standstill. The great heart that had beat for so many years in the Review and Herald building had stopped, and the entire institution felt the loss.

R. F. C. had come into the building by this time and he and I left immediately for the sanitarium. How different from the trip the day before! Now the issue was decided. Hope was gone. We were silent and somber. The elevator

14

seemed slow and listless, the air hushed. On the third floor of the san, as we tiptoed down to the little waiting room, we saw the brokenhearted group who had gathered—Mrs. Nichol; Virginia (Saxon); M. L. Tompkins, associate pastor of the Sligo church of which F. D. N. was a member; L. H. Pitton, public relations officer for the sanitarium; and Mrs. Evelyn Delafield, sanitarium Bible worker. Elder Tompkins was praying that the Lord would bring strength and comfort to Mrs. Nichol and Virginia at this moment of desolation, and would guide in the future of the work to which F. D. N. had given his brilliant, consecrated life.

Silently we joined the mourning group. Whispering words of condolence, we approached Mrs. Nichol, whose calm, strong faith did not waver. Bravely she refused to flinch even before this great sorrow.

Elder Figuhr and others appeared shortly. All spoke "words of comfort." But what can you say under circumstances like these?

When the first necessary decisions had been made, the little group separated, going their several ways.

I must tell Miriam, I thought. Twenty minutes later I knocked on her classroom door. When she answered the knock at 12:50 P.M., she knew instantly that something was terribly wrong. Never before in her years of teaching had I interrupted a class. And never before had I just stood, choked with emotion, unable to speak. At last I stammered, "Elder Nichol just died."

"No," she said, "you don't mean it." We talked for a few moments, then she suggested, "I still have ten more minutes of this English class, then we'll talk further. Sit down in the back of the room until the bell rings at 1:02. I have a thirty-minute lunch break then."

After relating the whole sorrowful story, which occupied the entire lunch break, I went home where I could be near the telephone. If Mrs. Nichol should want my help in any way, I wanted to be accessible.

Early in the afternoon Mrs. Nichol asked a friend to telephone me, suggesting that I meet her and Virginia at the funeral home about three-thirty. I was just getting ready to leave for the twenty-minute drive when Miriam came in, having cut her teaching day short.

"I'll go with you," she volunteered. "Perhaps I can make myself useful, or run errands, or contact people, or just anything."

At the funeral home Mrs. Nichol turned to me, simply and unaffectedly. "Will you take charge of the arrangements? My husband felt so close to you. He thought of you almost as a son."

Swallowing the lump in my throat, I responded, "I'd consider it a great honor, Mrs. Nichol."

Immediately I began to organize my thoughts. There were several factors to consider, primarily the fact that most of the General Conference men would be leaving Takoma Park by the middle of the following week, in preparation for the pre-sessions of the General Conference. They would, of course, wish to be present at F. D. N.'s funeral. Many overseas workers were in Takoma Park too, en route to General Conference. Some of them had never seen the editor of the *Review;* they had planned to see him in Detroit. Now they would want to attend his funeral.

Turning to Mrs. Nichol, I asked hesitantly, "Would Monday be too soon? I fear that if we wait any longer many of the men will be leaving."

"Whatever you consider best, we will do," this gracious lady answered. And Virginia concurred.

The next two days at our home were long and intense. It was my strong conviction that the funeral should reflect the kind of man F. D. N. was, that it should be impressive, even

211

majestic. I also felt, with others, that the death of this great man marked the end of an era. The denomination would never again be quite the same. Therefore the funeral must be dignified. It must be inspiring. It must be stately. It must be organized perfectly, as befits a man who gave meticulous attention to details, a man who put a premium on careful organization.

At home again, we planned the entire funeral, step by step. The telephone was our most useful tool. During the next forty-eight hours we placed and received endless calls. For hours on end the telephone rang instantly each time we put it down.

Mrs. Nichol suggested various people to take part in the funeral. There was Elder Theodore Carcich, then vice-president of the General Conference for North America. He had to be reached at "camp meeting somewhere in Louisiana." There was Elder Arthur White, close associate with F. D. N. in the White Estate, to be contacted "at Andrews University, I think." There was H. D. Singleton. And Elder Figuhr, providentially at home, who, without hesitation, agreed to preach the sermon. There was the thirty-four-voice Review and Herald Men's Chorus. Could they sing two numbers on short notice? Their director, M. E. Dawson, treasurer of the Review, after a moment's reflection, said, "Certainly we can do it!" And so on and on. F. D. N.'s pastor—W. A. Loveless—would he be back from the Potomac camp meeting? The church to be arranged for—Sligo. Organist—Don Vaughn.

In planning for the pallbearers, I felt that as many editors and writers should be included as possible. Mrs. Nichol concurred, so with the exception of Elder Neal Wilson, then president of the Columbia Union Conference, all the active pallbearers fell into that category.

Honorary pallbearers, we thought, should consist of members of the Review board, consulting editors of the *Review*

212

(vice-presidents of the General Conference), the White Estate trustees, plus personal friends whom Mrs. Nichol suggested. More telephone calls. Endless lists. Revisions. Corrections. For two days we virtually forgot about food and sleep.

At the funeral home F. D. N. lay in a mahogany casket, as handsome in death as in life, the room filled with floral sprays from individuals and institutions all over the world. That a man who was seldom alone in life should be alone in death was unthinkable; so we worked out a list of loving friends who stayed and received the scores of mourners who came to pay their respects. The funeral home guest book reads like a list of "Who's Who in the Seventh-day Adventist Denomination."

Through Saturday evening, and through all of Sunday they came. Particularly touching were overseas delegations, brought in by friends who were bilingual. My wife and I stayed at the funeral home Saturday evening, along with Merwin and Josephine Thurber. Through Elder W. E. Murray, who translated, we talked to workers from South America. Through other missionaries, we talked to workers from Japan, from India. We mourned together, for grief is a universal language.

In the midst of all the grief and planning had come the autopsy report which contradicted F. D. N.'s firm "diagnosis." Death had come from a ruptured aorta, or dissecting aneurysm, not from a "coronary," or heart attack.

Monday came. Could everything be ready by one-thirty in the afternoon? Harassed beyond words, I breathed many a silent prayer. Both editorial secretaries and others were pressed into service, typing and retyping lists and my tribute to F. D. N. composed under pressure the night before. R. F. C., peerless researcher, had been working tirelessly on an accurate life sketch. More telephone calls. More inquiries.

And then it was noon. The plant, with the flag at half-

213

mast, closed. The more than 300 employees filed out. The massive presses were silent. The proofroom was empty. The copyroom was deserted. The editorial offices, untidy as a result of the flurry of planning, were put in order and abandoned. F. D. N.'s third floor—his ivory tower—seemed to join in mourning.

At the Sligo church, hundreds of people were filing in. The parking situation was as complicated as we had feared; but people uncomplainingly walked for blocks. Inside, there were the flowers—acres of them, it seemed. There was the closed casket, with the beautiful casket piece of yellow and bronze chrysanthemums, lovingly sent by "The Family." There was the organ, being played softly and reverently. But most of all, there was the sense of bereavement, the feeling that something unique in the lives of the people there, and in the life of the Seventh-day Adventist denomination, was gone.

Before going on with the story, I would like to point out that at the time of F. D. N.'s death the *Review* schedule had been readjusted in preparation for the General Conference session. The regular weekly issues that were to precede the conference had all been published. The next *Review* would be dated June 16, and that would be the first General Conference Bulletin. Thus unless a "special" were published there was no way for the *Review* to report F. D. N.'s death to subscribers all over the world. What was to be done?

R. F. C. and I talked the situation over with C. E. Palmer, Theodore Carcich, and others. It was decided that an Extra should be issued to carry the story of F. D. N., his life, his death, and his funeral. This would be difficult but perhaps not impossible. Already the plant was set for General Conference Bulletin production. To create, publish, and mail an added number of the *Review* at this point would require something extra on the part of everyone. But the entire plant seemed to feel that the project should be undertaken. And so

FINAL SERVICES FOR A FALLEN GIANT

it was. The Extra was published. In it, the story of the funeral was told by H. M. Tippett, associate book editor at the Review. We are including it here.

"At one o'clock on Monday, June 6, the parking places serving Sligo church were at a premium and little groups of people were wending their way from every direction into the sanctuary. Among the estimated 1,300 at the service were businessmen and members of the community of other faiths whose friendship and respect for the deceased had been won during his nearly 40 years of residency in Takoma Park.

"While the people were quietly filling the pews, Donald Vaughn, Sligo church organist, was at the console of the pipe organ, softly playing hymns of faith and confidence that comfort grieving hearts. At 1:15 Arthur Walters, director of the Takoma Funeral Home, led the honorary pallbearers to their reserved seats at the right front of the church. Among the 30 who were present were representatives of the Review and Herald board, the staff and board of the White Estate, and members of editorial staffs, past and present.

"On the other side of the sanctuary the 34 members of the Review and Herald Men's Chorus were seated with their leader, Merrill Dawson, and accompanist, Giles Roberts. As soon as the mourning family took their seats in front of the bier, the officiating ministers occupied their places on the platform.

"To open the service the Men's Chorus sang the beautifully moving song: 'To See Thy Face.'

" 'Someday the plan divine, which now perplexes,
Ah, let me see and kiss those hands, nail riv'n.
And I'll remember through th' eternal ages
Thy life, dear Lord, for my poor life was giv'n.

" 'To see Thy face! To see Thy face!
Someday, not distant, Lord, I'll see Thy face!'

A large concourse of grieving friends accompanied the family to the last resting place of the beloved church leader F. D. N. to whom the tributes of this book were written as a memorial.

"Elder William Loveless, pastor of Sligo church, read Scripture portions that from time immemorial have comforted God's people in their hours of trial and grief, of triumph and exultation. The familiar phrases fell comfortingly upon every ear and brought memories of individual experiences to each believing heart.

"Elder Theodore Carcich, vice-president of the General Conference for North America, followed with a prayer that was full of earnest petition for God's gracious remembrance of His people, for angelic ministry to the bereaved, and for implementation of the promises of Heaven to the church in these solemn times. 'Thou whose mercies are from everlasting

216

to everlasting . . . fill our minds with the expectation of reunion at the coming of our blessed Lord.'

"The life sketch . . . was read by Elder R. F. Cottrell, associate editor of the *Review and Herald*. The break in his voice testified to his affection for the fallen leader.

"Elder Arthur L. White, secretary of the Ellen G. White Estate, spoke of his association with Elder Nichol, who for some years has been chairman of their board. He especially emphasized the undeviating defense of the writings of the Spirit of Prophecy by the deceased, and of his interest in plans for the ever-widening distribution of the counsels of the messenger of the Lord to His church.

"No more appropriate song could have been selected for the occasion than that sung so beautifully by Mrs. E. H. Atchley, accompanied on the organ by Mr. Vaughn, 'Is It Far to Canaan's Land?'

> " 'O the way is long and weary,
> And our trembling feet are sore;
> Is it far to Canaan's land?
>   *   *   *   *   *
> " 'O how sweet would be a resting place
> A safe and quiet home; . . .
> Where the cruel days of bondage
> And of fear will never come.
> It's not far to Canaan's land.'

"Elder Kenneth H. Wood, long associated with Elder Nichol and with his staff, suddenly charged with funeral arrangements and emergency plans for the paper, worked far into the evening hours preparing a fitting eulogy for this memorial service. That he was able to put together so eloquent a tribute . . . shows how close his sentiments were to his daily consciousness of the character and worth of his editorial chief.*

---

* See Appendix P for this tribute.

"The sermon by Elder R. R. Figuhr, president of the General Conference, was no stereotype of funeral occasions. He spoke with deep sincerity of the seemingly irreplaceable loss that had come to the church in the death of one of its most prominent leaders of thought and faith. Elder Nichol was always in close conference with Elder Figuhr on matters of great issue concerning the work and problems confronting the church. This loyalty of the *Review* editor to the cause and to its leaders was of frequent reference during the ceremonies. And no pen was more able to analyze the issues and present them in cogent form, urging all to rally around noble principles, than was that of this fallen leader.

"The Men's Chorus sang a song much loved by the deceased and couching in poignant phrases the hopes and aspirations of all who love the Advent message:

" 'We journey to a city which eye hath never seen;
We journey to a country whose shores are ever green. . . .

" 'No eye hath seen its glories, its joys have ne'er been told;
No cloud of sorrow passes above its streets of gold.'

"Elder H. D. Singleton, secretary of the North American Regional Department, and with whom Elder Nichol had been closely associated recently in the study of human relations, offered the closing prayer, most appropriate and benedictory, before the recessional led by the honorary pallbearers, the officiating ministers, and the active pallbearers.

"With the organ playing softly in the background, the hundreds of sorrowing friends filed past the open casket for a last look on the face of him whose name will ever be a revered memory. The honorary pallbearers formed a double row down the church steps while the casket was carried between the two lines. The active bearers were: B. B. Beach, educational and Sabbath school secretary of the Northern European Division; W. T. Crandall, editor, *Youth's Instructor*; R. R. Hegstad,

FINAL SERVICES FOR A FALLEN GIANT

editor, *Liberty;* Lawrence Maxwell, editor, *Guide;* M. R. Thurber, book editor, Review and Herald; Neal C. Wilson, president, Columbia Union Conference [now vice-president of the General Conference for North America].

"With the flashing warning lights of an escort of Takoma Park police, the funeral procession wended its way from Flower to Central Avenue, back to Carroll and out across New Hampshire Boulevard to Riggs Road, the mile-long cortege intersecting and halting mainline traffic everywhere.

"At George Washington Cemetery graveside services were conducted by Elders Carcich, Loveless, and White. If any message could come from the tomb, no admonition to us who remain would better express Elder Nichol's counsel than the hymn that was Winston Churchill's charge to Britain at his death:

> " 'Fight the good fight with all thy might,
> Christ is thy strength, and Christ thy right;
> Lay hold on life, and it shall be
> Thy joy and crown eternally.' "

"God gives to every man the virtue, temper, understanding, taste that lifts him into life and lets him fall just in the niche he was ordained to fall."

—WILLIAM COWPER

CHAPTER 17

Epilogue

SADLY I returned to F. D. N.'s office. I looked it over carefully, even as I had ten and a half years before. On the far wall still hung the fearsome devil mask from New Guinea. On the wall closest to his desk still hung the numerous pictures of Near Eastern Biblical ruins. At my right was the souvenir shield from the Philippines, covered with miniature swords. Next to the high-backed chair that he had used for so many years still stood his cube-shaped swivel-type bookcase.

I glanced down at the desk. A yellow lead pencil lay on a tablet on which he had been writing the General Conference *Review* schedule. Everything was exactly as this great and good man had left it as he went home for the noon hour.

Emotion almost choked me as I reflected on the mutability of life. F. D. N. had had no intimation that he was laying down his pencil for the last time, and that another hand would have to pick it up. He was a realist; he knew that this would happen eventually, but neither he nor anyone else had the remotest idea that it would happen so soon.

Ten days after his funeral the 1966 General Conference session convened in Detroit. As had been customary for many years, the *Review* published a daily Bulletin to report the proceedings of the conference. This is not the place to describe in detail the highly complex procedures involved in putting the *Review* on a daily-paper basis. I must, however, refer again to the fact that for the Detroit session the *Review* used TWX machines for the first time. Our *Review* office in Washington was connected directly with our temporary office in the motor city, by TWX. F. D. N. had arranged for this. He had looked forward to seeing the system in operation.

Remembering this, there was a lump in our throats as the news clattered out of our Detroit office on its way to Washington. We could not help thinking how much pleasure F. D. N. would have received from being in the midst of all the excitement. He always loved the tension and pressure of the General Conference session. He would have loved this one even more because of the dimension added by the TWX machine.

Immediately after the General Conference session, at a joint meeting of the Review and Herald board and the General Conference Committee, I was asked to pick up the editorial pencil that F. D. N. had laid down. As I write these lines, in January of 1967, I sit in the office where my close friendship with F. D. N. began more than eleven years ago. I sit here trying to visualize my predecessor's life from the perspective of a contemporary historian. What were the major contributions of this great man, to the world and to the Seventh-day Adventist Church?

Without making any attempt to place his achievements in the order of their importance, I should like to mention several major ones.

First, by the quality of his preaching F. D. N. added stature to the Adventist pulpit. By his keen, incisive thought and vigorous presentation he held the attention of audiences and inspired his hearers to quicken their steps along the pathway to the kingdom.

In recognition of his pulpit skill, Atlantic Union College, in 1960, inaugurated the Francis David Nichol lectureship on preaching. On a folder announcing the lectureship in 1961 appears this statement: "The lectureship was inaugurated in

EPILOGUE

1960 by the man whose name honors this series—Francis David Nichol, currently editor in chief of the *Review and Herald*, general denominational organ of the Seventh-day Adventist Church.

"A modern monarch of the pulpit, Doctor Nichol's name stands for artistry, versatility and persuasion in the royal task of interpreting God to man."

To achieve this eminence, F. D. N. paid the price in hard work. He had a brilliant intellect, an enormous vocabulary, and stage presence, but he did not depend on these alone. He believed in the value of hard, painstaking effort. He believed that this gave the Holy Spirit maximum opportunity to make his witness effective.

He always wrote out major addresses. With great care he sought for just the right word, the appropriate figure of speech. Patiently, he produced well-turned phrases. Endlessly he re-examined his logic and sequences, to increase the thrust of his message. Often he worked on a manuscript right up to the moment he was to present it, at times making changes even after he was seated on the platform.

The fact that he was always in demand as a speaker is clear evidence of his greatness in the pulpit, a greatness that was one of his major contributions to the Church.

The contemporary generation lives in a world where Adventism is a respected faith. Yet only a few years ago the picture was vastly different. Adventists were considered peculiar; their doctrines and ways were ridiculed.

That Seventh-day Adventists today are, in general, looked upon with respect is doubtless due, in part, to the work of F. D. N. His ardent defense of creationism during the 1920's, while not putting the evolutionary advocates to rout, at least made them realize that their theory was less than proved, and that their so-called "facts" may be interpreted in more ways than one—even by the creationist to support his own position.

223

Later, in the early 1940's, he turned his attention to the Millerite movement and wrote the influential book *The Midnight Cry*. With his customary thoroughness in searching out the facts, he traced down the stories that had been used for one hundred years to discredit the Millerite movement. One by one, he discovered that these tales could not stand the light of investigation.

Once and for all, he laid to rest the story that the Millerites had dressed in ascension robes, preparing for their Lord's return. So carefully did he document the facts that even the *Encyclopaedia Britannica,* which for years had carried the ascension stories in its account of the Millerite movement, altered its write-up and left out this bit of folklore. Other influential journals and books followed suit. Occasionally ascension-robe stories still appear in various publications, but the fact that they have been eliminated almost entirely from serious works is due largely to the work of F. D. N. It is one of his major contributions to Adventism.

In the field of medicine F. D. N. likewise left a significant legacy. Though he was not a physician, he was widely respected in medical circles. No doubt this was due partly to his skillful, energetic work as editor of *Life and Health* magazine. When he became editor of this ailing journal, the circulation hovered around 26,000 a month. He built it up to more than 200,000, and by absorbing another health magazine its circulation reached about 260,000.

But circulation figures tell only part of the story of F. D. N.'s interest in medicine. He believed wholeheartedly in the philosophies of medical work outlined in the writings of Ellen G. White. He believed also that a close relationship exists between a healthy body and a healthy soul. As a result, he worked untiringly as an apologist for our medical program, and was ever alert to keep faddists and fanatics from discrediting our health reform message.

224

EPILOGUE

As editor of the *Review* he felt a solemn obligation to protect church members not only from religious heresy but from medical heresy. Thus during the mid-1950's when Harry M. Hoxsey, of Dallas, Texas, was receiving widespread publicity for his cancer "cures," F. D. N. presented in the *Review* "An Examination of the Claims of the Hoxsey Cancer Clinic." His conclusion was that in the light of the best scientific evidence, Mr. Hoxsey's claims to cure cancer were unprovable at best, and fraudulent at worst.

Some *Review* readers took issue with F. D. N. not only over his conclusions but over the right of the *Review* to become involved in a current medical controversy. F. D. N. explained his position by saying: "We have had a special reason for doing this rather extended piece of investigation. We have discovered that a remarkably large number of people think that the Hoxsey Clinic might hold hope for them. We have therefore felt it a public duty to present our findings at some length. Early detection and prompt, adequate treatment of cancer are perhaps the most important factors in assuring maximum hope of cure. If a supposed 'cure' does not cure, then the patient has lost precious time that may finally cost him his life. We are interested in the physical, as well as the spiritual, lives of our subscribers."

Apparently F. D. N.'s presentation was both scientific and defensible, for the medical profession endorsed it without reservation. The American Cancer Society ordered 10,000 reprints. Later Government authorities were quoted as saying that the careful case that F. D. N. built helped contribute to the eventual downfall of Mr. Hoxsey's program.

This, of course, was only one aspect of the contribution that F. D. N. made in the medical field. Consistently, through the pages of the *Review,* he encouraged calm, scientific investigation of the principles of health reform advocated by the church. For himself, he accepted without reservation the coun-

15

sel given by Ellen G. White concerning healthful living. He knew, however, that some fellow Christians felt the need of scientific undergirding for their faith. He wanted to provide help for these people.

To his credit let it be said that although he accepted Mrs. White's writings as inspired, and acted without hesitation on her counsels, he was never judgmental in dealing with those who found it less easy to believe. He was convinced that the revelations given through Ellen G. White were entirely in agreement with science, and he sought continually to show the harmony between the two. His faith-and-intellect approach helped place our health program in a position to command the respect of the scientific world.

No summary of F. D. N.'s contributions would be complete without mention of the *Seventh-day Adventist Bible Commentary*. Few men have the courage to undertake a project of this magnitude. Fewer still have the ability to carry it through to successful completion. F. D. N. had both. When the project was initiated, some people feared that the dangers of the assignment were greater than the possible benefits.

F. D. N. saw clearly the perils. He saw that rigid dogmatism in the explanation of texts and doctrines that could be understood in different ways would produce sharp division within the church. He carefully avoided this pitfall. Instead of presenting a single interpretation, he offered all of the major interpretations, leaving it to the reader to adopt the one that seemed most reasonable, in the light of the facts.

His policy of having the Commentary material read in galley form by a large number of Bible students throughout the world made it clear that neither he nor the Review and Herald Publishing Association was endeavoring to determine denominational doctrinal beliefs, nor freeze our teachings into a creed. F. D. N. felt that the Commentary should reflect a broad spectrum of denominational thinking; it should be truly representative. The fact that the Commentary has received enthusiastic acceptance and has helped unite the church, instead of divide it, reveals clearly the wisdom of his plan.

F. D. N. had a clear conviction that the Commentary should represent the best in modern scholarship. He was determined that the content of these volumes would command the respect of serious Bible students and researchers everywhere. He did not expect that all would agree with certain of the interpretations, but he felt that they would at least recognize that the positions set forth could be defended.

Thus through the Commentary project F. D. N. gave Adventism new stature in the scholarly world. We think that this, combined with the help that the Commentary has brought to Adventists everywhere, is one of his major contributions.

Leaving now the world of F. D. N.'s literary contributions —and I have not even mentioned most of his books*—I would like to focus on a quality of his character that revealed itself in every aspect of his life. F. D. N. was dedicated to the pursuit of excellence. He was never satisfied with the ordinary. To him the "I can get by" philosophy was positively repugnant. In his writings he was not satisfied with prosaic, unimaginative words and phrases. He was always looking for a better way to say things, a better way to do things.

One writer has said: "Some people may have greatness thrust upon them. Very few have excellence thrust upon them. They achieve it. They do not achieve it unwittingly, by 'doing what comes naturally'; and they don't stumble into it in the course of amusing themselves. All excellence involves discipline and tenacity of purpose."

This was true of F. D. N. If his example can serve to inspire others to pursue excellence with the same single-minded determination that characterized him, perhaps this will be his greatest contribution.

---

* See Appendix A for complete list.

HIS INITIALS WERE F. D. N.

So deep an impression has this man made on my own life that even as I write these lines I cannot help wondering what his reaction would be if he could read over my shoulder. It wouldn't surprise me if he would shake his head sadly and say, "Young man, you've just lost fifty points!"

Even so, I'd welcome the sound of that voice. It would seem so right to hear it again in this office where my friendship with F. D. N. began, on a raw, windy day early in November, 1955.

APPENDIXES

Appendix A

PUBLICATIONS BY F. D. N.

Books

The Answer to Modern Religious Thinking, 1936
Answers to Objections, 1932, Revised 1952
Behold, He Cometh, 1938
The Case Against Liquor, 1944
Certainty of My Faith, 1948
Creation—Not Evolution, 1926 (Coauthor with Alonzo Baker)
Ellen G. White and Her Critics, 1951
God's Challenge to Modern Apostasy, 1935
If Bombs Fall! 1942 (Paperback)—Compiler and Editor
Letters From Far Lands, 1948
Let's Live Our Beliefs, 1947
Making Ready for Heaven, 1938, 1947
The Midnight Cry, 1944
Questions People Have Asked Me, 1959
Reasons for Our Faith, 1947
San Francisco Debates on Evolution by Maynard Shipley, 1925
The Seventh-day Adventist Bible Commentary, 1953-1957—Editor
Signs of Christ's Coming, 1931
Why I Believe in Mrs. E. G. White, 1964 (Paperback)

Pamphlets

A Century of Our Health Message and Why Seventh-day Adventists
   Operate Hospitals, 1964
The Denominational Significance of the College of Medical Evan-
   gelists (An address at the Second Development Conference of the
   College of Medical Evangelists, Sabbath, March 16, 1957)
The Genius and Scope of Our Medical Work, 1949
In the Name of Common Honesty
Restudying the Doctrines Without Destroying the Foundations,
   1939
The Story of the Lost Day, 1930
Two Addresses on Health, 1961
Wet or Dry, 1932
Why I Am a Seventh-day Adventist, 1943

229

Appendix B

F. D. N.'S TRIBUTE TO FRANCIS MC LELLAN WILCOX

(Read at Elder Wilcox' funeral and published in the Review, *Sept. 13, 1951.)*

This is no attempt to present a life sketch of Elder Wilcox, which will cover many years and many activities. That will appear later. This is a personal tribute to a great and good man of God, who was called to his rest on August 30.

Elder Wilcox lived a long life, eighty-six years. Never in robust health, often beset by afflictions, he made up in spiritual resources what he lacked in physical. For one third of a century he was the editor of the *Review*. His time of editorship added to that of James White and Uriah Smith, spanned almost one hundred years from the founding of the journal in 1849.

It was my privilege to know him intimately for twenty-four years. Eighteen years of that time we labored in adjoining offices. I knew him when he worked under pressure that would have tested the poise of a saint. I knew him when he carried on despite physical pain. I knew him when his soul was mightily stirred to write on grave and far-reaching issues that confronted the movement. And so this pen portrait, inadequate though it be, is not drawn with the shadowy hand of hearsay or colored with the falsely flattering tints of dim memory.

Elder Wilcox was a man of great convictions. He stood for something. He kept the faith. To guard and to promote Adventist beliefs and standards was to him more than an editorial duty, it was a passion. No subtle speculations tinctured his writings. No question marks punctuated his declarations on doctrine.

But he was singularly free from that pride of opinion, that rigidity in thought and position, that so frequently weakens the witness borne by men of strong convictions. Not only did he love God and the message; he loved his brethren also. A sweet reasonableness distinguished his discussions in committees. A large elasticity of soul enabled him to revise, and even to reverse, his view when the weight of evidence went against it. He did not suffer from the delusion that has affected some good men, that his original position on a question was infallibly right. How much greater might be our harmony if all of us could only realize that our viewpoints often need the correction that can come from discussion.

He was a man who lived his beliefs. There was no jarring discord between his profession and his practice. He radiated simple, unaffected piety. It was a piety neither funereal nor cloying. Rather it was serene and benign. He even enjoyed a little pleasantry. He was human in a heavenly sort of way. Once in a committee, of which he was chairman, he made a remark that his sensitive spiritual nature led him to feel was not as kind as it should have been. The next day each member of the committee received a personal letter from him expressing his sorrow and asking forgiveness. What better proof of true greatness or of genuine Christianity can anyone provide than that! He was the kind of man you would call to pray for you if you lay mortally ill. And how often he was thus called! He was the kind of man to whom you would naturally turn for wise and sympathetic counsel in an hour of perplexity or darkness. And how often his counsel was thus sought after!

He was a man of great compassion and solicitude for those in sickness, sorrow, or adversity. And as with Job of old, the cause which he knew not he searched out. He was a frequent visitor at the bedside of the sick. It was his custom, after a special prayer for someone, to write him the next day a letter of hope and courage in the Lord. Even in the years of his retirement, when he learned of a death in the home of some worker in Takoma Park, he would write to our editorial office for the street address of the family that he might send them a letter of sympathy.

He was a man wholly devoid of ostentation and vain display, both in dress and in deportment. His quiet and almost retiring manner seemed to belie the inner strength he possessed. He provided constant proof that great force of character may tabernacle in an apparently passive soul, and a wholly unpretentious exterior may conceal great personal power. The impressive record of his life should give pause to those who, seeking to make their mark in life, attempt to acquire so-called dynamic personalities or to dazzle men with their glittering skills.

One of the clearest revelations of a man's character is the manner in which he treats those who work with him and under him. It is no small accomplishment for a man to labor for a third of a century within the four walls of one institution, holding ever the respect and the love of all his associates and leaving with their unfeigned expressions of Christian affection as a benediction to his public life. That was Elder Wilcox's accomplishment. What does it avail a man to tell of his great exploits and successes if the conference committee must tell him to move to a new place of labor because those who have worked for him are no longer willing to work with him? A thin veneer of sanctity is not sufficient. The constant frictions of life, including rubbing shoulders day after day with the elect, will wear through a veneer and expose the base metal beneath. Elder Wilcox's religion was not skin deep; it permeated his whole being.

When he retired he gave to us who followed him his patriarchal blessing and his sympathetic cooperation. He stepped down from office of his own volition, declaring that his race was run and that younger hands and hearts must carry on. Throughout his sunset years he sought not to dictate or direct, but only to speak words of encouragement to those carrying the work that for so long was his. I visited him on a number of occasions during those years, and thought each time of the poet's words:

"In the eyes of a young man, fire;
On the brow of an old man, light."

On his brow was the light of heaven, a reflection from the throne above toward which he daily turned his face. By that light he walked, and by its mellowing rays he was made ripe for the garner of God. Our visits together always closed with his request: "Won't you offer a word of prayer?"

It is hard to compress in a sentence his distinctive contribution to the Advent Movement. It was not a contribution of compelling eloquence that swept men off their feet, though he was in truth a pleasing speaker. Nor was it a contribution in the field of government, though his counsel was ever desired and much respected in administrative committees. Rather, his unique contribution was his presentation of the beliefs, the standards, and the objectives of the church with that peculiar persuasiveness that flows from deep conviction and with that singular authority that springs from a blameless life.

And now he has died, full of years and full of the grace of God. But we sorrow not as do others who have no hope. In the midst of our grief we rejoice, for our hope is in Him who brought life and immortality to light through the gospel.

Appendix C

F. D. N.'S TRIBUTE TO J. L. MC ELHANY

(Published in the Review *of July 23, 1959. The tribute was written while F. D. N. was on a world trip.)*

This is my first opportunity to write a tribute to Elder McElhany. Only yesterday (July 2) I received the sorrowful tidings in Berlin. Eulogies of some men are hard to write. Their lives seem short of the kind of deeds and words that stimulate one to adorn their memory with flowers. Not so with Elder McElhany.

Office taints some men—makes them cold, calculating, political. Beyond all doubt, office discloses the real stature of the man.

232

APPENDIXES

Some it exposes as dwarfed souls, little and petty; others it reveals as tall, expansive, largehearted and lovable. The latter describes Elder McElhany, who held the highest office in the church for 14 years. I am sure of this not from hearsay and perfunctory contacts but from some 40 years of growing acquaintance, which ripened into sweet fellowship. I think it not unseemly to say this, for such fellowship should ever be within the range of those who love their Lord.

Elder McElhany might most aptly be described as an exhibit of a man of high ideals in high office. He combined the qualities of an able administrator and a warmhearted, pious man. Too often one of these two qualities dominates an official's life to the dwarfing of the other. In Elder McElhany there was no dramatic or colorful display of either quality. He was the quiet, urbane kind of Christian and official who must have given the angels little or no distress as they recorded what he said and did.

There were relaxed moments when he revealed, by the turn of a phrase, that he was delightfully human. I loved him for that. Perish the thought that a sense of humor is sinful. Most times, however, he radiated gravity and quiet dignity. That was his unfailing mood in public. I respected and honored him for that. The leadership of the Advent Movement is a grave assignment.

No trace of impatient haste seemed ever to reveal itself in him. Indeed, his calm and measured manner almost deceived a few into thinking him irresolute and unimaginative. The record provides the proper evaluation of him. I have often looked at that record, in the context of the whole record of growth and expansion of the movement for a century. No apology need be offered for the 14 years he served as president. On the contrary, those years stand forth brightly. His was the leadership during the last 5 bitter years of the great depression, and the even more bitter years of the war that followed. Heaven assigned to him one of the most difficult and bewildering periods in the history of the Advent people. One hasty, ill-advised move during any of that time might easily have had disastrous repercussions for our work over the whole earth.

Elder McElhany was not a spectacular or impetuous man. Men who do display those tendencies, I've often thought, must embarrass the great God who patiently and quietly seeks to lead the Advent Movement to the kingdom. Good sense and ripe judgment seem rarely to display themselves spectacularly. Our beloved brother seemed to tune in on the quiet, measured wave length of Heaven as he carried on his public work.

But let no one think that he lacked courage to express deep

233

and explicit convictions in critical hours. None ever had reason to feel that he wavered on vital issues, especially those that affected the great doctrines and standards of the faith. Perhaps he held two committee meetings on a problem, when some might think one enough. I well remember what he said to me in just such an instance: "We must give ample opportunity for everyone to express his mind if we are to hope finally for genuine unity in our decisions." Evidently he must have well succeeded in generating a spirit of unity. Only thus can we explain his repeated election to high office. Certainly no one ever hinted that he gained election by political endeavor.

You needed to talk with Elder McElhany only a little time to feel that he was an old-fashioned kind of Adventist in the most wholesome meaning of that phrase. Free of the taint of fanaticism, but firm in his conviction that we must stand stoutly for some things, he brought confidence to all.

Elder McElhany always had to husband his physical resources. But he gave freely of himself to those in distressing situations. One night, in Washington, after he had come from his office, weary with endless committees, and facing more on the morrow, a young ministerial student knocked at his front door. The student was in deep trouble. Personal problems had combined with spiritual doubts to plunge him into great mental distress. Elder McElhany did not send him to his local pastor. He became a pastor of souls himself—ever the minister's highest function—and spent the evening talking with him. This incident—unpublicized, except on the record above—was typical of our beloved brother.

On more than one occasion there were strong-minded men in committees who opposed his plans, occasionally, I felt, with unnecessary vigor and tenacity—we are still in our earthly state. I commented on this in speaking with him in private one day. His reply is still bright in my memory: "The goal of a leader in God's work is to learn how to live peacefully with those who differ with him." And then when I pressed him with an illustration of one brother, who, I felt, had been more than robust in his comments on a measure under consideration, his only reply was: "Brother ——— is an honest man."

How significant it is that though public officials naturally presume they will be rated by posterity in terms of some major act or program they have executed, their rating is more generally in terms of some of their apparently minor words and deeds. The explanation, of course, is that these so-called minor things often provide the most dependable measure of men. So it was with Elder McElhany. The insights that various off-the-record incidents provide reveal him to have been the kind of man the world and the cause could ill afford to lose.

I last talked with him some eight months ago. It was my practice regularly to call on him when I came to California. The visit closed with a season of prayer—one of those seasons when you feel that the gracious God has drawn very near to bless and to warm your heart. We rose to our feet. He brushed a tear from his cheek, placed his arm about me and said: "Brother Nichol, I love you." Thus we came to the moment of parting. More than once I've thought of that beautiful moment when Heaven seemed to draw so near. I think of it now. I shall always cherish it as one of the sweetest of my memories—the memory of one of God's great good men who could say simply and spontaneously, "I love you." His was truly an "unfeigned love of the brethren." Dear Lord, give us more such men.

Appendix D

CITATION OF F. D. NICHOL BY CHARLES E. WENIGER
MAY 22, 1958
AT THE CONFERRING OF THE DOCTOR OF DIVINITY DEGREE

President Dick: The Candidate whom I have the pleasure of presenting to you to receive an honorary degree from Potomac University, is Francis D. Nichol. Born in Australia, he was graduated from Pacific Union College in 1920 with the degree of Bachelor of Theology, began his pastoral-evangelistic activities in California, was ordained in 1923, served as associate editor of the *Signs of the Times* for six years, became associate editor of the *Review and Herald* in 1928, edited *Life and Health* 1934-1946, and has held his present position as editor of the *Review and Herald*, official church paper of Seventh-day Adventists, since 1945.

He is author or coauthor of fifteen volumes, contributor to numerous scholarly and religious journals, and a speaker of significance at professional and academic conferences.

As a lecturer in the Seventh-day Adventist Theological Seminary since 1936, Mr. Nichol has shown himself an ardent protagonist of an educated ministry. As an assiduous scholar he has displayed depth of theological acumen, indefatigable zeal, and a habit of meticulous research, culminating most recently in his leadership as editor in chief of the *Seventh-day Adventist Bible Commentary*.

In recognition of the candidate's theological competence and his dedication of life, tongue, and pen to the work of the Seventh-day Adventist Church, I present to you, President Dick, on behalf of the Board of Trustees and the Faculty of Potomac University, Francis D. Nichol as the recipient of the honorary degree, Doctor of Divinity.

Appendix E   May 22, 1958
RESPONSE OF F. D. NICHOL TO THE CITATION BY DR. C. E. WENIGER AT THE GIVING OF THE DOCTOR OF DIVINITY DEGREE

Mr. President, learned schoolmen, august trustees, colorful graduates, ladies and gentlemen:

As I have listened to ministers at funeral services voicing fulsome eulogies that went even beyond hyperbole, I have thought: How unfortunate that Adventist theology prevents the deceased from hearing the adulatory adjectives. But any abnormal interest I might have had consciously to attend my own funeral has been more than satisfied this evening. And, may I note, learned schoolmen evidently claim the same license in expression as do ministers. I am sure that my beloved friend, Dr. Weniger, who is a master of English, will pardon my embarrassed reference to the poetic license that he has just seen fit to display in describing an old schoolmate of his. Having heard such kind and colorful words, perhaps I should say, as did Simeon of old: "Now lettest thou thy servant depart in peace."

But all pleasantry aside, Mr. President, I wish to say that I am deeply moved by the gracious act of the Potomac University in bestowing upon me this degree. It is both unexpected and undeserved. I feel deeply honored to be an alumnus of this university, and assure you that I shall give to it my strong support in the days that are ahead.

On an occasion like this it is hard to refrain from historical review. Some eighty-five years ago we founded our first school of higher learning, the Battle Creek College. The founding was certainly not an endeavor to find an outlet for surplus church funds, for the school was begun in the midst of grinding poverty. Nor was it launched because of any lack of schools of higher learning in the country. The explanation for the creation of that first college, and all our other denominational schools since then, is found in this fact: We believe that the education of our youth is the most important task of the church, and that true education requires a certain synthesis of the heavenly and the earthly, a certain training of heart and mind together.

No church can justify its separate existence except in terms of distinctive beliefs and standards, and these can be perpetuated only as they are made an integral part of the curriculum and atmosphere of the schools in which the youth of the church are educated. Seventh-day Adventism is synonymous with a certain way of life, a particular view of God and the supernatural. Our schools are the repositories and the guardians of that way of life and of this distinctive view.

There have been those among us, who, because of intellectual sloth or lack of willingness to sacrifice, have felt no need of higher schools among us. As if the evils of secular, godless education could be successfully met by ignorance and illiteracy. God gave us heads and He intended that we should use them. I believe that higher education may be sanctified to the glory of God.

It may surprise some to know that Mrs. White, in making an appeal in 1889 for the higher education of our ministry, declared: "We have had altogether too much talk about coming down to the common mind. God wants men of talent and good minds, who can weigh arguments. . . . These men will be able to reach, not only the common, but the better classes."—*Testimonies,* vol. 5, p. 581. It was none other than James White who long ago poured scorn on the idea that because we expect the early advent of Christ we can therefore neglect education. He declared that Adventist ministers ought to be the best trained men in the world.

Perhaps there are some, still, in our ranks who wish cavalierly to dismiss the whole matter of higher education by quoting Solomon's observation that much study is a weariness to the flesh. Perhaps! But the minister who does not study much soon becomes a weariness to the flesh of everyone who must listen to him.

Before the Potomac University, latest and most significant of all our educational institutions, lies a great future. It was created in faith and spiritual travail. Its doors open, now, to the youth of the Advent Movement. To you who direct the affairs of the university comes the delicate and difficult task of maintaining high scholastic standards while avoiding the blight of bleak intellectualism. True education is more than the marshaling of clammy facts, or the drafting of impeccable hypotheses. Do not let this university become an intellectual deepfreeze. Through its halls should ever blow softly the vitalizingly balmy and fragrant breezes from the valley of Eden.

God bless the Potomac University and its dedicated personnel.

Appendix F

COMMENTS ON F. D. N. BY PRESIDENT OF AMERICAN MEDICAL ASSOCIATION

Review and Herald Editor, Francis D. Nichol, was unexpectedly lauded by Edward R. Annis, M.D., president of the American

Medical Association and of the World Medical Association, at the October 25 meeting in Washington, D.C., of the National Congress on Medical Quackery.

The following remarks were made by Dr. Annis after F. D. N.'s invocation:

"Ladies and Gentlemen:

"I think you should know more about the gentleman who delivered the invocation just before lunch. This was Dr. Francis D. Nichol, Editor of the *Review and Herald,* official organ of the Seventh-day Adventist Church.

"Dr. Nichol has been known to those interested in the battle against medical quacks for more than thirty years. Dr. W. W. Bauer of the AMA staff, who will participate in a panel this afternoon, writes of him:

" 'I have known Dr. Nichol for more than thirty years. I used to look forward to his visits with pleasure, because he always had stimulating and interesting matters to discuss. As Editor of *Life and Health,* he was not content to sit in his swivel-chair and let articles come in "over the transom." He traveled widely to meet his contributors, and developed articles out of ideas discussed with his authors in their offices. His little notebook was always filled with notations about whom to consult where about what.

" 'His hair has been white ever since first I knew him, but his boundless energy and zest for life seem to make him ageless. I cannot see that he has slowed down appreciably in the third of a century since he first came into my office, when I took him to lunch and asked him if he could make a vegetarian luncheon in a meat-eating environment. "Certainly," he said. "I've been doing it all my life. I never tasted a bit of meat, and when people sympathize with me, I tell them I feel sorry for them—they needn't feel sorry for me."

" 'The publications for which he has been responsible have always stood for high standards, both scientific and ethical. They have been friends of medicine and foes of quackery, uncompromising and courageous, and where they have differed with other scientists, tolerant and courteous. Despite their vegetarian convictions, they have allowed me to say, in their pages, that poultry, meat and fish are the best sources of protein for most people.'

"Dr. Nichol is perhaps best known to many of us for his cooperation with the Food and Drug Administration in 1956, when he published the FDA warning against the Hoxsey cancer treatment. The net result was an avalanche of angry letters from readers. The challenge took him to Dallas and elsewhere, seeking the truth about the Hoxsey treatment. The result was a publication entitled

APPENDIXES

'Examination of the Claims of the Hoxsey Cancer Clinic,' published in the *Review and Herald* for Dec. 13 and 20, 1956. Reprints of this have been more useful as a source of information about the Hoxsey treatment, and have been widely distributed both by AMA and FDA.

"Dr. Nichol has also, in his past, exposed the Millerite myth of the 1840's. He wrote, also, an exposé of the hoax of flying saucers, and he warned his readers about guzzling vitamin pills as a cure-all as long ago as 1944. In 1938 he wrote 'The Revolt of a Secondhand Smoker' and 'A Formula for True Greatness.'

"In the circumstances, it is with great pleasure that we salute Dr. Nichol as a leader in the fight against medical quackery, and other forms of bamboozling of our great and gullible public!"— *University Scope*, Nov. 1, 1963.

Appendix G

A FEW F. D. N. STATEMENTS QUOTED IN MAGAZINES

Look, July 27, 1954

"The Rev. F. D. Nichol, Seventh Day Adventist leader, at a world conclave of that denomination: 'Higher education has not raised man heavenward; there are simply more college graduates in jail.' "

Life, April 19, 1954

"To those whose theology makes them impatient either for Judgment Day or for some evidence of human improvement, there seems to be an implied rebuff in what F. D. Nichol calls 'the endlessly increasing total of good men's tombstones.' These stones may or may not point toward God's final victory over sin and death; what matters is that in each case goodness was a personal achievement and heaven doubtless a personal reward. Like corals building the Great Barrier Reef, all these Christians created our Western civilization as the unplanned by-product of their personal hope and labor. Simple piety tells us not to despise such a by-product; but if we really wish to defend and extend it, to make it a 'continuing city,' we can do so only by imitating the builders, whose real hope was elsewhere."

The Chaplain, June, 1954

"Francis D. Nichol, after taking on both modernism and neo-orthodoxy (*Christian Century*, Feb. 10), sharpens the issues with Dr. Van Dusen:
" 'Many churchmen in America contend that their view of the

future "does not deny the possibility of Christ's return to end history. But it does not believe this expectation to be an *essential* element in Christian hope for the world." Their view affirms faith in "God's sovereignty" and "the certitude of the complete triumph of his purposes for history." But because the "hope for each Christian's future beyond death centers in the assurance of eternal life with Christ," this view "finds no need and no intelligible meaning for a fulfillment of the corporate life of mankind other than the incorporation of all which merits preservation in the eternal Kingdom of God above and beyond the stress and turmoil, the advance and retrogression, of humanity's pilgrimage in time and on earth." (See *Christian Century,* Nov. 25, 1953, page 1357.)' "

Information Service, Saturday, April 3, 1954

"The doctrine of the second advent can hardly be avoided by the Second Assembly of the World Council of Churches at Evanston, writes Francis D. Nichol, an editor of the official magazine of the Seventh-day Adventists, in *The Christian Century,* Chicago, Ill., February 10, 1954.

" 'Most Christians, until our modern day, have seen the solution of the problem of a sorry world in terms of the return of Christ,' writes Mr. Nichol. 'Scientists now say that world annihilation may be upon us shortly.' 'The second advent doctrine has ever stood, not as a vague synonym of God's sovereignty, but as a definite declaration of how the will of God will be carried out.'

" 'In a day when earth's annihilation is easily possible, a complete rethinking of modernist premises is imperative. An immanent God is inadequate to meet the threat of imminent catastrophe. The orderly action of nature's laws is unable to cope with the disorderly action of human nature. Only a transcendent, personal God, only a miracle-working God, can measure up to the world's need. In such a conception of God the biblical doctrine of the second advent makes sense.' "

Appendix H
REMARKS AT THE FUNERAL OF PROFESSOR C. W. IRWIN

(In the Takoma Park Church, August 2, 1934, by F.D.N.)

It is undoubtedly true that students in a school cannot long conceal from their teacher their real selves. What they actually are soon stands revealed. Especially is this true in a boarding school, where the teacher can observe the words and actions of his students during the whole cycle of the day's activities. It is equally true, I believe, that the teacher cannot long conceal his real self from his students. He is ever the object of critical attention and comment, particularly if he be the head of the school.

For this reason, if for no other, I feel prepared to speak with certainty a word regarding Charles Walter Irwin. I think of him always as Professor Irwin, for it was my privilege to receive my college training under him. My memory of those years is vivid. I recall critical moments that arose, as they always will. I recall, too, the deadly routine that must inevitably mark most of the days, the monotonous grind of a thousand recurring duties and contacts that fill the life of one who is a school head. Looking back over those years, and with no shadow of mental reservation hiding any detail of the picture, I see no instance where my beloved college president, by word or deed or expression, fell short of my youthful ideal of a gentleman and a Christian. That is saying a very great deal, for the ideals of a youth are high, and few reach or long remain on the lofty pinnacle he has mentally reared.

I think of Professor Irwin as an old-fashioned man, in the choicest sense of that word. He had an old-fashioned view of simplicity in life. No atmosphere of ostentation or affectation surrounded him; it never occurred to any of us in college to hesitate to approach him. Yet with the simplicity went a dignity that drew from us a deep and wholesome respect. It was the kind of dignity that is built on the framework of the more rugged and homely virtues. He taught us to be gentlemen at heart as well as in manner.

He had an old-fashioned view of the social relations that should be maintained between the sexes. Impetuous youth often indicted him for this. But the great majority of us rise up today and call him blessed for maintaining an atmosphere most conducive to study and character development, and most free from those enervating social influences that so constantly seek to press in on a school group.

He had an old-fashioned view of the true dignity of labor. He preached that manual labor is honorable, and he practiced what he preached. There is indelibly impressed on my mind the picture of Professor Irwin, in laborer's clothes, working on the grounds with a company of students. He gave to us a balanced view of the importance of the hand and the head. No training could better have aided us in learning the difficult art of keeping our feet on the earth while our minds dwelt in the sky.

He had an old-fashioned view of the Advent Movement, of the reasons for the existence of our schools, of the confidence that should be placed in the inspired instruction that had been given

16

in the writings of Sister White. With faith in his heart and a pickax in his hand he carved a college out of a hillside in the Far West. One with less faith in the Spirit of Prophecy would not have attempted it. Pacific Union College is a standing monument to his pioneering spirit and his absolute confidence in the divine leadership of this people. Someone has said that an institution is but the lengthened shadow of a man. Pacific Union College is the lengthened shadow of Professor Irwin. And, protected by that shadow from the fierce light of skepticism regarding this movement and all religion that so often blinds their eyes, many young men and women have walked safely out of school into the world.

In behalf of a host of youth whom he has trained, and prepared for useful lives, I reverently say, with full realization of the meaning of the words, Thank God for Professor Irwin!

Appendix I

**A TYPICAL PRAYER THAT F. D. N. GAVE TO PEOPLE
WHO WANTED TO PRAY BUT FELT
THEY DID NOT KNOW WHAT TO SAY**

Dear Lord, Thou who hast promised to be a Father to the fatherless, and a Husband to the widow, I come to Thee in simple faith, confident that Thou wilt hear me, and wilt give me an answer to my prayer. I come to Thee in utter sincerity, for I long above all else to do Thy will. I thank Thee, first, for the blessing of life and of health. I thank Thee for the ideals that Thou hast implanted in my heart, the standards of right and wrong, and the active working of a heavenly-stimulated conscience. But, dear Lord, the world, the flesh, and the devil assail me. In my own strength I am unable to fight successfully the battle of life. But I claim Thy promise that with every temptation Thou hast prepared a way of escape, and that I can be more than conqueror through Jesus Christ who loves me.

I am resolutely determined by Thine enabling grace to lead the kind of life that will give me inner calm, a sense of fellowship with Thee, and a confident sense of respect in the eyes of all with whom I associate. Dear Lord, my goal is heaven. Send a tall shining angel to walk beside me and to guard me. I thank Thee that Thou hast heard me. I walk confidently into the future with Thee, claiming all things through Jesus Christ my Lord. Amen.

Appendix J

**A TYPICAL LETTER WRITTEN BY F. D. N. TO A
YOUNG MAN FROM THE HYATTSVILLE, MARYLAND,
CHURCH, WHO WAS ENTERING NATIONAL SERVICE**

APPENDIXES

November 28, 1943

I wanted to drop you this little line before you leave for the war tomorrow. It is quite a day in your life. No one but you can fully appreciate it, because you're the one that's going through it. But I wanted you to know, Vernon, that we are thinking about you, and we're going to keep thinking about you after you have gone, because you're one of our boys.

I remember you very well when you were still in the kindergarten. That's quite a while ago. I have always thought of you as part and parcel of our life in the Hyattsville church, and I still do, though up to this moment you have not been baptized and joined the church in a formal way. I believe this is something you will want to consider doing at the earliest opportunity, Vernon, because it's the right thing to do, and gives the public witness to all the world of what you stand for. That's what the Bible says we should do.

Here's the real point now that I want to make in writing this note. You have been reared in a Christian home and according to certain standards. You know these are right and you want to follow them. And, what's more, it's possible to follow them, Vernon, even though you'll be among a lot of men who may not love God or the Bible. It all depends on what kind of stand you take at the very beginning. You don't have to be stuffy about it nor look extra pious, nor be a killjoy as the boys say. You can be happy and normal and yet stand squarely for some principles and ideals in which you believe. And when you do that men will respect you. It's really remarkable how men do respect anybody who has some real convictions and who stands for them, and when you do stand for principles, Vernon, you'll find after a while that the kind of young men who stand for the same principles will like to associate with you. You know it's still true that birds of a feather flock together. There are always a number of young men who want to stand for very real, good things, and when you have such associates you'll find it still easier to stand for the good things. The important point is always to stand at the very beginning. Never hesitate, never stall. It's what you do when the first situation develops that determines a lot how you will get along on the next situation and every other situation after that. Always be most respectful and deferential to the officers, but yet clear in the statement of the principles in which we believe. That applies to the matter of working on the Sabbath, and in the matter of bearing arms. Almost every army camp in the country today is well acquainted with our Adventist principles and has made allowance for them, but just

243

the same each young man going in generally has to make his personal statement of conviction before he receives consideration. Then sometimes a new officer will come in command of a camp, and you must do it all over again. But the point is never to waver on your convictions. Convictions aren't any good at all unless you stand on them, and when you are standing on convictions you're on pretty solid ground. You will find after a while that not only the men around you will respect you, but your officers will respect you also because of your principles.

There are times when you'll be homesick, Vernon. Every boy is. There are times when you'll wonder what it's all about. The air will be a bit foggy around you, but remember we've all gone through experiences more or less like this when we have been thrown out into the world for one reason and another. Yet the good Lord has carried us through the experiences and we are stronger because of them. And most of us, Vernon, never really knew that there was very much of value or substance to religion or praying to God until we did get into a hard spot. I think that's one of the reasons why God allows us to get into hard spots. So I want to suggest to you, Vernon, that you begin really working at this matter of religion in a very practical, simple kind of fashion. When you start out for the army, start out on the plan of talking to God in the morning when you get up, and to God in the evening when you go to bed, and reading something from the Book of God. Just talk to God like you'd talk to a father, asking Him to guide your steps for the day and to give you wisdom and good judgment and to enable you to stand for principles that you believe in. It's surprising, Vernon, what it does for a fellow. It gives him courage to speak up when he needs to speak up. It gives him courage to stand for some things that he might not otherwise stand for. It's a simple formula. In fact, it's so simple that a lot of young men really don't know how valuable it is until they get into a very hard place, but I want you to remember it. It's just a parting suggestion from someone who has watched you grow up to young manhood and who has had your interest very much at heart. . . .

Now God be with you, Vernon. We are counting on you to stand as a fine, clean young man, radiating out good, wholesome principles and Christian ideals no matter what part of the world you find yourself in. We're going to pray for you. We believe in you. Success to you on your journey, and may you come home safe to us again.

Sincerely,
F. D. NICHOL

APPENDIXES

Appendix K

TYPICAL LETTER WRITTEN BY F. D. N.
TO A HOSPITALIZED FRIEND

Mrs. R. F. Woods
Kindness of M. R. Thurber

August 24, 1964

DEAR EVELYN:

I am in California and have just learned over the telephone from Washington of your grave illness and surgery. I understand that it was a week ago today. This shocks me and makes me feel distressed. If I were at home, of course, I would be coming over to the hospital to see you. The best I can do at long range is to remember you in my prayers, and that, of course, I will do. May the dear Lord graciously hear all our prayers in the way that we want them heard. Of course, we cannot demand of our God. We can only appeal. Let us be thankful that He always will listen with compassion.

Now here is hoping, wishing, and praying that the dear Lord will soon lift you up. My very kind thoughts and sympathies also to your beloved husband.

FDN s

Most sincerely,
F. D. NICHOL

P.S. I still remember the days when you were the most efficient secretary of the PUC Alumni Association.

Appendix L

TYPICAL LETTER WRITTEN BY F. D. N.
TO A BEREAVED FRIEND

December 16, 1965

Mrs. Darlene Sherrig
Newbury Park Academy
Newbury Park, California 91320

DEAR MRS. SHERRIG:

Lucile, whom I used to know long ago when I was stationed out West and when her father was living, has written me of Harry's death, and thus of the great tragedy that has befallen you. Of course, I am wholly unacquainted with you and with your sweet little family. In fact, I had completely lost track of Harry for quite a number of years. My first and really vivid memory of him was of a fair-haired, blue-eyed, and very erect little boy five years old, standing beside the bus that I was boarding at Union College in Nebraska. The picture is still vivid in my mind. A sweeter little boy I have never known. It was a temptation just to stow him in my suitcase and go off with him—for I have always been a lover of boys and girls. The years hurried by and I made, I believe, not more than one or two contacts as he grew up. I talked with him once on the telephone when I was in San Francisco, I think it must have been about ten years ago. I urged him to come over to the big meeting that I was reporting, but somehow we didn't get together. And then came the shocking news from Lucile that he was dead.

How quickly the years hurry by, bringing little boys to manhood, to fatherhood, and sometimes to death. If he continued to have the sweet qualities of childhood—and I like to think that he did—you must have had a very wonderful husband and his children a very wonderful father. And now he is gone. How feeble and faltering are words when we try to express our feelings as we stand at the portals of eternity. I am not going to attempt it, Darlene. I am simply going to say that I sorrow with you and send with this letter all of the sympathy and compassion I possess, plus a little hug and kiss for Buddy and for each of your two sweet babes.

I am not wise enough to understand all the ways of God. I am sure He lives and that He has an ultimate purpose for all of our lives in this little world. I can never bring myself to feel that His infinite purposes for us are confined to the short years of our earthly life, which leads me confidently to believe that God has plans for us beyond this life. And this belief is buttressed by what the Holy Scriptures tell us. I realize how hard it is for us to feel that a good God still lives and guides even though He permits tragedies to come. But then, Darlene, we are not wise enough to know what is best for us in a divine plan that affects us for all eternity. There is a place for quiet trust and simple faith to believe that God doeth all things well. Almost all of us have had this test of faith in one form or another during our lives. Most of us have stood, at least once, at the grave of a dear one, as he was committed to the earth.

We are tempted to feel, when we stand in the deepening shadows, that the sun has gone down forever. But it hasn't. The sun always rises again on a new tomorrow. It will for you also, for God has not deserted you, and certainly God never intends that any of His children should walk forever in darkness. There will in time be streaks of light on the eastern horizon and the warmth of color, accompanied by the songs of birds once more. I can only say to you, as you stand in this darkness, lift up your head, the stars are still there, each one guided unfailingly by a Divine Hand, the same Hand that will guide and steady you, till the morning comes and the light shines warmly and beautifully again.

You will have found, then, that somehow, mysteriously, during the period of darkness, sorrow, and sad memories, dear Harry has moved, in the perspective of your mind, from someone whom you expect should be walking beside you down the lane, to someone clothed in light, who has been transported to a world of beautiful memories, memories that are real and heavenly, memories that no longer have in them the sharp pain that they once had. Time is not only the divine anesthetic, it is also the divine aid to a readjustment in our picture of the beloved who have left us. It will take an exercise of faith for you, at this moment, to believe what I am saying, but please do, for I am saying the truth.

Now, during the hours of darkness and shadows, of hollow sounds and tormenting memories, lift your heart quietly to your God and talk with Him. A strange calm will come over you, an inexplicable quietness, and a strange strength for your feet as you go forward. And besides, may the Lord of all peace, who loves little children, protect your three.

FDN s

Most sympathetically yours,
F. D. Nichol

P.S. Enclosed are two little pieces of literature that might be helpful to you.

Appendix M

EXCHANGE OF CORRESPONDENCE BETWEEN
F. D. N. AND C. S. LEWIS

May 27, 1959

Dr. C. S. Lewis
Cambridge University
Cambridge, England

DEAR DR. LEWIS:

I remember with pleasure my interview with you in 1950 at Oxford. You said that when I came through the next time to let you know ahead so that it would be possible to give me a little more of your valuable time.

I shall be in the vicinity of London July 6 to 15. I'll be lecturing in the morning to a college, but most every afternoon I will be free—except, of course, one or two afternoons when I will be seeing some dignitary. But those particular afternoons I cannot at this moment know. If you would be kind enough to drop me a line before I leave the United States on June 11, letting me know how I might reach you by telephone, I could then phone you on July 6 to discover what day and hour would be agreeable to you.

Thanking you in advance for your great kindness, I remain

Sincerely,
F. D. Nichol

247

HIS INITIALS WERE F. D. N.

June 2, 1959

Magdalene College
Cambridge

DEAR MR. NICHOL:

I am not at all sure where I shall be between July 6 and 15. The telephone addresses to try are Oxford 62963 (this is the more probable) and Cambridge 59457. It wd. be nice if we could meet.

Yours sincerely,
C. S. LEWIS

Appendix N

TYPICAL SHORT ARTICLES BY F. D. N., PUBLISHED ON THE BACK PAGE OF *SIGNS OF THE TIMES* IN 1921, THE FIRST YEAR F. D. N. WAS ON THE STAFF

Almost unbelievable are the reports coming through the press dispatches, of the trial for murder of a child eleven years of age. It is true that the jury disagreed; but the mere fact that there was sufficient evidence to cause a number of the jury to believe this child guilty of the awful crime is strong presumptive evidence that the charge is not unfounded.

Be that as it may, the case is but typical of a situation confronting our land to-day. Young men in their early teens are being convicted of crimes ranging from petty larceny right up to the capital crime of murder itself.

Only a short time ago, the writer was speaking with one of the wardens of the San Quentin Penitentiary. In answer to a question regarding the age of most of the convicts admitted, he replied that of late years mostly young men had been coming through the iron gate. A scrutiny of the faces of those within altogether confirmed this old warden's astounding statement.

Such conditions do not bode well for our country. The young men of to-day are the controllers of the nation to-morrow. But simply to lament conditions cannot improve them. The root of the difficulty must be reached. All possible reasons for such increases in the criminal activities of the youth must be examined.

Since the old adage, "By beholding we become changed," still holds true, here are two suggestive lines of investigation: The "movies," with their infernal gun-play adorning every act, and their scenes of robberies and murders and worse; and popular fiction, with its warped moral standard.

F. D. N.
July 12, 1921

Exit Common Sense

A wit once said that common sense is the rarest thing in the

248

world. The humor lay in the paradox. But there is sadness as well as humor in it.

In all walks of life, the absence of common sense is painfully noticeable. Perhaps our very highly organized system of society is partly responsible. We have specialists for each line of work. We are not qualified all around. The newspapers are a sad commentary on this.

But most unfortunate of all, the rarity of good, old-fashioned common sense is affecting us in matters of religion. Strange cults and isms are legion to-day. They teach strange doctrines, the like of which has never been heard of before, except, perhaps, in the wilds of some heathen temple. Their vaporings have to do with imaginary auras, and projected thought waves. One labors to prove the nonexistence of the only thing known to exist—matter; while another endeavors to establish the actual existence of the one thing which common sense has always told us does not exist—a spook.

Theories and hypotheses regarding life and all religion which neither Paul nor angels ever heard of are being agitated throughout the country. They fill bulky magazines which declare themselves to be organs of the "new light," or of the "inner circle," or of some other mystic organization.

But strange as all this is, and hard as it is to believe that such theories could ever formulate themselves in the mind of an individual, there is one thing still harder to believe; namely, that such notions should meet with such ready reception on every hand.

The whole thing might take on the aspect of a farce and be banished from the mind with a wholesome laugh, were it not for the fact that it has a very serious side. The good solid religion of our forefathers, the balance wheel of the past generation, is being exchanged for these chaffy theories and isms. One must be exchanged for the other, for the two cannot exist together in one mind.

Views and beliefs which, according to the Bible, we have long believed to be false and evil, are being advocated by various cults as correct and harmless. The apostle Paul speaks of those who, in the last days of the world's history, are running after all the deceptions which the prince of darkness has formulated. He says that "for this cause God shall send them strong delusion, that they should believe a lie." If men do not desire to receive the Bible, which is the "truth," God, who will not restrict man's freedom of will, is going to let them accept lies which bring as a result, "damnation."

F. D. N.

July 12, 1921

HIS INITIALS WERE F. D. N.

Balloon Weddings

"Preacher marries couple with the aid of wireless, as they float high aloft in a balloon," reads a headline of the morning's paper. A perusal of the account discloses that a love-smitten pair contrived a novel way of getting married; namely, ascending in a balloon, and then having a minister, seated at a wireless station on the earth, ask them the stated questions and receive the time-honored replies.

Now, far be it from us to impugn the motive or to question the good intentions of this couple. But we certainly do feel to raise our voice against the general laxity noticeable in connection with the marriage ceremony, of which this case is illustrative. So long as we are human, we will modify our ideas of things by the company and associations in which we find them. Our idea of billiard playing, for example, is a rather poor one, due primarily to the fact that we are forced to associate with it many features that are objectionable. And so with many other things.

This principle is working out in regard to some of the most sacred institutions of life. Marriage is being associated with questionable romance, fantastic nuptials, salacious scandal, and easy divorce. It is being made the mine from which punsters, comic writers, and stage wits draw to replenish their stock in trade. The effect has been that marriage to-day is viewed in a strange light.

There is need that saner and holier associations be formed about the word. This can come about only as the whole question is viewed in a different light, and with a great deal more seriousness. The balloon ceremony well typifies the present view of marriage: something airy, to be tossed about by any passing wind of fancy. To all who view marriage in the light that this balloon couple do, we would say, both literally and figuratively, Come down to earth.

F. D. N.

July 26, 1921

Dogs or Babies

Two most extraordinary clippings recently came into my hands. They revealed the existence of a most unusual state of affairs. One clipping reads thus: "$8,000 Left Poodle for Meals and Bed. Rex is only a poodle, 7 years old, but for the rest of his life he will take his meals sitting at the table in a high chair, will sleep in a regular bed, and will have a Christmas tree, lighted with candles, each year. This is assured him by the terms of the will of Mrs. Rose E. Porter, who left $8,000 to be used in caring for the dog as she designated."

250

APPENDIXES

The other clipping is very similar. Beneath a news photo which shows a well-dressed woman holding a blanketed dog in her arms, are these words: "Mrs. Sidney A. Williams of New York, with her pet, 'Snoopie,' who recently arrived from Europe. 'Snoopie,' weighing exactly a pound and a quarter, upon arrival, sported a hood and cloak especially designed, which protected him from the Atlantic's icy winds. Mrs. Williams values the dog at several thousand dollars, and refused to sell her pet when the Prince of Monaco made an offer for the tiny black and tan at Monte Carlo."

These news items reveal a condition which has long-existed in this advanced and highly civilized land of ours. It is not a condition which has arisen in the past few months. And this opens before us an interesting comparison. An examination of the dates in connection with the will of Mrs. Rose E. Porter shows that it was drawn up at the time when the awful famines were raging both in Europe and in China. It was drawn up at a time when the daily, weekly, and monthly papers of the whole country were publishing heart-rending stories about these famines under the powerful caption: "Ten dollars will save a life." By the American mind, which translates everything into terms of dollars, that caption could not be misunderstood. We were made to realize that squandering ten dollars on something worthless was synonymous with sacrificing the life of an innocent child in devastated Europe. In view of the national publicity given this whole matter and in view of the tangible form in which the appeal for aid was couched, none could plead ignorance of the tragedy, nor lack of comprehension of the means of remedying it. One hundred dollars meant ten lives, one thousand dollars meant one hundred lives, and eight thousand dollars, the amount named in that first clipping, meant eight hundred lives. Yet in view of all this, a human being, a woman, being of sound and disposing mind and memory, and enjoying full possession of her faculties, as the legal preface to a will declares, did publish and declare this to be her last will and testament; to wit, that $8,000 of her fortune should be dedicated to the work of providing meals and shelter for a dog. And at the close of that will, she placed her signature. Oh, the horror of the thing! a legal document transformed into an instrument of destruction; a woman signing the death warrant of eight hundred innocent children.

But that is not all. Think also of that woman who recently arrived here from Europe with her "Snoopie" all swathed in warm blankets. She had come from the very land where there are to be seen on every hand poverty, hunger, and dirt; where precious babes by the thousand are to be found whose faces are so emaciated

251

HIS INITIALS WERE F. D. N.

with hunger that they look like haggard old men; and where there is such a scarcity of clothing that infants in the hospitals, instead of being wrapped in soft, downy blankets, are bundled up in rags and newspapers. She had come from a land filled to overflowing with wreckage from a world catastrophe,—sightless, armless, and legless men struggling desperately to provide food and clothing for their families. She had come from a land filled with widows and orphans whose plight is too pitiful to relate. She passed through a land where death stalks on every side, and where the cry of anguish and the heart-breaking appeal for help arose as one sad chorus.

But she shut her eyes to the sights and her ears to the cries, and rode brazenly through that valley of the shadow of death with a dog in her arms. Loving caresses that would have brought a smile to wan baby faces were bestowed upon a dumb brute; warm raiment that would have kept the biting cold from some baby form were thrown about the body of a beast; and nourishing food that would have brought back life and vigor to a famine-stricken soul was prostituted to satisfying the appetite of a dog.

But still again. Gaze upon the accompanying picture. A charity worker endeavors to sell the services of a strong, bright-looking young man. No one bids. No one desires to give him work or to aid him in his distress. The auctioneer puts up a dog, and is bid $5. Not one cent to help a man, but $5 for a cur; a dog of more value than a man! What can such things mean? What does such a state of things portend? The Bible prophet declares that "in the last days" men would be "without natural affection." (2 Timothy 3:1-3.) Surely we have reached the "last days" of this world's history, for we have to-day the spectacle of a dog preferred to a babe; a cur, to a human soul; and that is *unnatural* "affection."

F. D. N.
October 25, 1921

Appendix O

PRECIS OF F. D. N. DEVOTIONAL MESSAGE

(Prepared for presentation at the 1966 session of the College and University Bible and Biblical Languages Teachers Section Meeting, Andrews University. It was read posthumously.)

I am talking only to a segment of our teachers, but a most important one. In fact, I can think of no more important reason for the existence of our Adventist schools than to teach our youth religion. And for those youth who plan to be ministers, I can think of no subject that is much more important than that of Biblical languages. True, we don't need a knowledge of Hebrew or Greek in order to have fellowship with God, but those languages do en-

252

able us to have a warmer, more understanding fellowship with Isaiah and Paul, for example.

To this group of teachers, so interlocked in their interests and objectives, I would say, above all else, and in the language of Paul: "Preach the word." All else is secondary. We take the historic position that Christianity is a revealed religion and it is revealed in a book called the Bible. Make your presentation of the Scriptures significant both for the head and the heart of your students. Only thus will they, in turn, be able to make the Holy Book truly significant to their parishioners.

Beware of any tendency toward presenting the Bible primarily as a great study in literature. It is that, but much more. I remember traveling by plane in Europe alongside the first secretary to the Spanish Embassy in France. When he learned I was a minister, he exclaimed: "I'd like to have been a minister." When I revealed some measure of amazement, he explained, immediately, "I'd like to teach Greek." When I continued to look a bit amazed, he said, "The writings of Paul are such beautiful Greek. I could become enthusiastic about presenting the Bible as a great piece of literature." But from other things he said on that flight I had to conclude that the Bible was to him simply a piece of literature and not a guide to holy living.

Help your students to realize that though logic and argument have a very valid place, they are tools that must be used with caution and always secondary to the presentation of truth on the plane of the heart and the spirit. . . .

Beware of ultra-intellectualism. It tends to make of your classroom a kind of intellectual deepfreeze. . . .

Always seek to build certainty into the minds of your students. There are too many people who are inclined to travel in their religious thinking around the dangerous curves of question marks. They are the descendants of those of whom Paul spoke: "Ever learning, and never able to come to the knowledge of the truth." It is your prime business to present to your students those things which are most surely believed among us.

Remember, you ever deal with great mysteries when you deal with religion and salvation. Don't try to explain in detail everything in the area of mysteries, such as the Trinity and the incarnation. Don't pose as understanding fully the mystery of inspiration, for example.

You who are the teachers of those who are to become the ministry of the Advent Movement have a task freighted with immeasurable potential for weal or woe. You can make or break the Advent Movement in a generation.

Appendix P

A TRIBUTE TO FRANCIS DAVID NICHOL

By Kenneth H. Wood

(Read at F. D. N.'s funeral, and published in the Review Extra, *June 10, 1966.)*

It requires the perspective of time to provide an accurate evaluation of the life of a man, and to assign him his place in history; yet even now, immersed though we are in sorrow and surrounded by the dark clouds of death, it takes but dim eyesight to see clearly that Francis David Nichol was a great and good man. He was great in physical vigor, great in intellect, great in human emotions, great in deep convictions.

And all that was great about him he dedicated to the Advent cause. As a skillful editor and eloquent preacher he applied the total capabilities of his tireless energy and brilliant mind to the task of articulating clearly the unique purpose of the great Second Advent Movement. With a single-mindedness that sometimes mystified and awed even his associates, he proclaimed both the truths held in common with all Christian bodies and those Biblical insights that are God's special gift to the world through the Advent people.

He not only proclaimed those truths, he defended them with all the sanctified vigor and wisdom at his command. He felt called upon to be one of God's lawyers in a world where higher criticism and scientific discoveries had placed historic fundamental Christianity on trial for its life. That he made a strong defense for truth, no one can deny.

And what he preached he lived. He believed that the Advent message must go to all the world in a brief span of time, and he always did more than his part to undergird that advance by generous contributions. Most of his gifts were anonymous, but heaven's records will testify that they were not inconsiderable. Not only did he give to needs within the church, he gave to lighten the burdens of individuals. His fiscal philosophy was that money is a sacred trust, not to be used selfishly but to benefit others. With the same type of thrift that characterized the pioneers of the Advent Movement, he lived frugally and unostentatiously in order to advance the cause. His life was a silent condemnation of the luxury and gadgetry of the affluent society. He never had a radio in his car, and only in recent years did he permit himself the convenience of an automatic transmission—perhaps due, I have sometimes thought, to excessive persuasion on the part of associates.

Elder Nichol lived the kind of Adventism that seemed both

reasonable and relevant in a twentieth-century context. He fought all forms of fanaticism, and even as he did so performed a successful marriage between faith and reason in his own life. Better than most people, he exemplified the beliefs of Adventism. I have often thought that if someone were to ask the question, "What is a Seventh-day Adventist?" I could hardly give a better answer than to say, "Francis David Nichol is a Seventh-day Adventist." Apparently this was not merely my personal opinion, for one of the many telegrams of condolence that have poured in since his death says, in part: "No one has served the cause of Christ with more devotion or with such fearless courage. He will long be remembered for his contribution to the church."

Some men shine with almost dazzling brilliance when before large crowds, but show up poorly in the person-to-person, day-by-day working relationships. This was not true with Elder Nichol. While he had few, if any, peers in public presentations, he was likewise exceptional in many traits that are revealed only behind the scenes. He expected his fellow workers to put forth their best efforts, but he understood that the human element is uncertain at best, and when mistakes were made he always accepted the full responsibility as editor. He never tried to shift the blame to others, never sought to hide behind lesser men.

Elder Nichol scorned sycophants but showed genuine admiration for men of sincere and sterling character. Frequently, for example, his love and profound respect for his predecessor, Elder F. M. Wilcox, cropped up in our office conversations. Often he spoke of Elder Wilcox as a saint, a man of God, a man of tact, a man who was well organized, who never procrastinated but always kept ahead of his work. It was apparent that, in many respects, Elder Nichol hoped to emulate his great and good predecessor.

In this he did not fail. Never one to leave assignments to the last minute, he had completed preparations for four speaking assignments next weekend at Andrews University. His major appointment represented about 40 manuscript pages. Likewise, he had completed all the preliminary organization for printing the daily Bulletins during the General Conference session. Eagerly he looked forward to the added excitement and exhilaration involved in producing a daily paper, as he liked to think of it, for distribution to the delegates at Detroit. He loved life and its attending pressures.

Elder Nichol was an extremely complex man, with many facets to his character. He had a keen sense of humor, and always had an appropriate story for every occasion, yet he had a dominantly serious side. He had a brilliant intellect, yet he did not retreat into the world of the mind; he was very much a part of the world about him.

HIS INITIALS WERE F. D. N.

No one who ever saw his eyes light up at the sight of a red-haired child or baby can doubt the genuine warmth of his nature. And no one who ever went to him in trouble—and there were many—can doubt his deep interest in helping to solve even self-caused problems. Not a few in our community will feel keenly that they have lost a sympathetic friend—one who not only listened willingly but who kept absolutely secret the confidences entrusted to him. And patients in the sanitarium will miss his visits, made voluntarily week by week whenever he was not out of town traveling.

But what can we say in such a limited time to give any adequate picture of this man who used his God-given gifts so unstintingly in the service of the One who gave them? Should we forget to mention that though he sometimes thought his brethren were mistaken in their decisions, he joined hands with them, so dedicated was he to the unity of the church? Should we not mention that he possessed such an abundance of natural talents that it would have been easy to grow more dependent on self and less on the Lord, yet he paused for short prayers at regular intervals during each day at the office, seeking wisdom and strength from Him who alone is the source of all things good? Should we not mention that his influence in the publishing house was so enormous that when news of his death passed like an electric shock through the building, small clusters of workers gathered tearfully here and there in the halls, unbelievingly, hoping for word that somehow the dreadful report was untrue?

Words cannot capture the essence that was Elder Nichol—the sparkle, the good humor, the rugged individualism, the mighty intellect, the deep spirituality. As the poet Browning wrote, ". . . all gifts which the world offers singly, on one head combine!" In our loss perhaps it would be appropriate to express our feelings through the famous literary passage borrowed for use in connection with the death of America's recent young President:

"When he shall die,
Take him and cut him out in little stars,
And he will make the face of heaven so fine
That all the world will be in love with night,
And pay no worship to the garish sun."

Speaking personally, I can only say that a giant has fallen, and like a towering tree in the forest felled by the woodsman's ax, his passing leaves "a lonesome place against the sky."